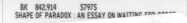

St. Louis Community College

Library

5801 Wilson Avenue
St. Louis, Missouri 63110

THE SHAPE OF PARADOX

Bert O. States

The Shape of Paradox

An Essay on *Waiting for Godot*

University of California Press

Berkeley · *Los Angeles* · *London*

University of California Press
Berkeley and Los Angeles, California

University of California Press, Ltd.
London, England

ISBN 0-520-03549-6
Library of Congress Catalog Card Number: 77-80478
Printed in the United States of America

1   2   3   4   5   6   7   8   9

for my sister Lois

Contents

I am interested in the shape of ideas even if I do not believe in them. There is a wonderful sentence in Augustine. I wish I could remember the Latin. It is even finer in Latin than in English. "Do not despair; one of the thieves was saved. Do not presume; one of the thieves was damned." That sentence has a wonderful shape. It is the shape that matters.

—SAMUEL BECKETT

I
The Language of Myth

My epigraph[1] is more than a poetic or philosophical perspective on my subject: it is the subject itself. My aim here will be to examine the respects in which the Augustine paradox imitates the "shape" of *Waiting for Godot*—is, in fact, a perfect working model of the play's structural dialectic.

I will be concerned in later chapters with the theological idea that is lodged in the paradox, but perhaps, for the record, it would be well to show its general relevance to the play. *Godot,* one might say, is about the two thieves, or rather about the idea posed by the parable of the two thieves. For we are dealing here not only with characters and events—say Vladimir and Estragon, who, as far as we know, have no such destiny as crucifixion (and all that follows)—but with the odds or "percentages" of salvation versus damnation for the race. In short, the two thieves who die with Christ are nothing more, or less, than momentary symbols of the theme that is the subject, in one way or another, of all the Scriptures. It is almost too awesome a theme to be dealt with outside the devotional sanctity of allegory, and allegory, as Beckett

1. I am using the version that first appears in Harold Hobson's "Samuel Beckett, Dramatist of the Year," *International Theatre Annual,* No. 1 (London: John Calder, 1956), pp. 153–155.

says in *Proust,* always fails in the hands of a poet.[2] Given the modern mood, moreover, it would even seem that Beckett the poet undertook it at a certain risk which lingers, one critical syllable beyond allegory, in the very title of the play. It is a big dangerous theme, this theme of themes. As Coleridge stunningly sums it up, "A Fall of some sort or other—the creation, as it were, of the non-absolute—is the fundamental postulate of the moral history of man. Without this hypothesis, man is unintelligible; with it, every phenomenon is explicable. The mystery itself is too profound for human insight."[3] Or, as Vladimir might say, "It's too much for one man." And that is the danger: it is almost too profound for "the boards." One cannot come at it with too secure a belief or it degenerates into doctrine, and, if justice is to be done to its profundity, one cannot come at it with too devastating an irony. What made Beckett the ideal modern to write a play about "The Fall"—as opposed, say, to Claudel, on one hand, or Ionesco, on the other—is that his peculiar skepticism of all firm positions rescued him (in this play at least) from both the artistic sin of Faith and the shallowness of an easy despair. Which is to say that he chose Augustine's paradox of the two thieves and not the moralistic version in Luke in which salvation and damnation are distributed on the basis of conduct (one thief reviled Christ and was, apparently,

2. *Proust* (New York: Grove Press, n.d.), p. 60.
3. *Table Talk,* May 1, 1830. This passage was called to my attention by Kenneth Burke in *The Rhetoric of Religion: Studies in Logology* (Berkeley and Los Angeles: University of California Press, 1970), p. 174.

damned; one confessed and was, apparently, saved).[4]
Hence that fascinating sentence—*it is the shape that matters*—standing provocatively beneath the mystery of the Cross.

Put simply, this essay is an examination of the ways in which shape matters in *Godot*. This comes down, mainly, to a problem of language and its function as an ordering principle of the play's master myth. In other words, I am not concerned with the *poetry* in the language or with an interpretation of the play but with the structure of its intelligibility. In some ways, the essay is an extension of a problem in poetics I dealt with recently in a study of *Hamlet:* that is, the way in which a

4. Like others, I have been unable to find the Augustine quotation, which may have appeared anywhere in the voluminous (and largely unindexed) body of his work. Most of the references in Augustine to the two thieves are direct glosses on Luke with no implication of paradox or doubt. However, if Augustine didn't write the sentence Beckett frequently quotes, it could certainly be said to coincide with his theology of grace. That is, for Augustine grace is not distributed on the basis of faith or confession, but through God's inscrutable will which we can never hope to understand: "If you understand, it is not God" (Sermon 117). I have located a passage in which at least one of the two thieves is cited by Augustine in the drama of presumption and despair: "Then the thief confessed, and at the same time Peter became confused. As the one bore witness the other denied Christ. But if God gained the thief, did he lose Peter, the denier? Far be it, far be it. He who paid the price [of our redemption] was performing a mystery, demonstrating in Peter's case that no just man should presume [*praesumere*], and in the thief's that no impious man, having confessed, may perish. Let the good man fear lest he perish through pride; let the evil man not despair [*desperet*] of his many wicked acts" (*"De Symbolo ad Catechumenos,"* *Patrologiae Latina,* Vol. 40, ed. J. P. Migne [Paris 1845], col. 646. My translation). This is scarcely a paradox, but it is more representative of Augustine's complex

fiction teaches us to fill in details that are not there at all and do so in the style of those that are.[5] What I was chiefly interested in was the thickness of *Hamlet's* world as communicated by the unusual diversity and density of its imagery, or what I called word pictures. This thickness, I suggested, has a significant effect on our options for interpreting the play; for it is primarily through imagery, or linguistically established "scenery," that we derive our sense of the qualitative range of a play's world, its limits and possibilities, the kinds of things that can take place in its spatial and temporal environment.

---

view of grace than the glosses on Luke 23: 39–43. It should be said that presumption and despair are often opposed in Augustine, with hope as the pious mean attitude between the two impious extremes—a conjunction which has interesting implications for the play, especially in view of Vladimir's quotation from Proverbs (13:12), "Hope deferred maketh the something [the heart] sick, who said that?" (Augustine on this verse: "God by deferring our hope, stretches our desire; by the desiring, stretches the mind; by stretching, makes it more capacious. . . . Let us therefore desire, for we shall be filled. Let us stretch ourselves unto Him, that when He shall come, He may fill us." See *An Augustine Synthesis,* arranged by Erich Przywara [New York: Harper & Brothers, 1958], pp. 77–78.) I am not sure how far one might carry this, but certainly Beckett was aware of the presumption-hope-despair idea as a possible approach to the play's theological problem. In any case, in this essay I will assume that the "wonderful sentence" Beckett quotes is, in spirit at least, Augustine's and not mis-remembered from another source.

I wish to acknowledge the generous assistance and advice of my colleagues in Medieval studies: Professors Thomas Hill, Winthrop Wetherbee, James J. John, and James O'Donnell.

5. "The Word Pictures in *Hamlet,*" *Hudson Review* 26, No. 3 (Autumn 1973): 510–522.

More recently, I used *Hamlet* as the central text of a seminar as a means of grounding certain principles of Shakespeare's art and dramatic art in general. It occurred to me that one way of illuminating *Hamlet*'s style (in the more inclusive sense of the word) would be to put it flat against the text of a dramatist who was working at the other stylistic extreme while treating similar thematic issues. In short, through the neutralizing effects of a double perspective we might minimize the risks of losing the unique sense of a writer in the familiar and seductive jungle of his own "closed" world.[6] With respect to style alone, the perfect antithesis of *Hamlet* is *Waiting for Godot,* the modern play, above all others, which seems to involve us in these same risks of overfamiliarity to an especially high degree—perhaps for the same reason that they run so high in *Hamlet:* that is, a certain archetypal richness which makes it all but impossible to read the play as anything but an icon of a permanent racial enigma.

What impresses one about *Godot* (in contrast to *Hamlet*) is the linguistic spareness of its world. Whereas in *Hamlet* a single image is apt to get lost in a crowded universe of images and to become significant, or thematic, through frequent variation and repetition, in *Godot* the image achieves an instant significance by virtue of occurring—and often only once—in an "empty" space, or one in which it obtrudes suddenly from a language texture composed of seemingly ran-

6. Hugh Kenner treats the subject of the artist's closed world, using Beckett as a key instance, in "Art in a Closed Field," *Virginia Quarterly Review* 38 (Autumn 1962): 597–613.

dom or diversionary conversation. It is this quality of randomness that creates the paradoxical impression of an unplanned design. In fact, if we were to condense *Godot* to a graphic illustration of itself, it might resemble a highly "successful" Rorschach blot.[7] I am not thinking of its possible diagnostic values or of a particular shape it might take (say, three vaguely crosslike forms); rather, I have in mind the simple wonder of the blot's appeal: like Found Art, it is unintentionally provocative; not a created object but a creative one, or better still, no object at all but a concatenation of possibilities, limited by nothing but the mind's capacity to endow shape with meaning. In other words, in the blot principle we confront the very algebra of imagination; in a flash of form we bypass the whole realm of factual equivalence and enter a world where structural affinity is the only law governing identity. This also happens to be the world of dreams and myth, and my more specific aim here is to examine the extraordinary mythic "pull" of this play from the standpoint of its formal allurements which, I would argue, are roughly analogous to the hide-and-seek artistry of the Rorschach blot.

To qualify the analogy a bit further, I am hardly implying that Beckett, or any playwright, could be unintentionally provocative with any success. What I

7. Others have used the Rorschach analogy in connection with Beckett's work. For instance, Hugh Kenner, *Samuel Beckett: A Critical Study* (Berkeley and Los Angeles: University of California Press, 1973), p. 66; and Vivian Mercier, *Beckett/Beckett* (New York: Oxford University Press, 1977), p. vii.

mean is that the shapes and subshapes in *Godot* behave *as if* they were. No sooner do we begin the play than we are in the presence of a massive duplicity which is at once the source of its peculiar openness and its resistance to interpretation. Everything has a way of meaning something and at the same time blurring any clear sign of representational intention. This is not simply the normal ambiguity of symbol systems but a kind of flatness or indifference in the text which provokes an extraordinary creative indulgence in the reader (a critical syndrome we might liken to Rapture of the Deep). The perfect novelistic parallel might be Kafka. Some years ago there was a book on Kafka which studiously traced Kafka's Oedipal obsessions through his imagery and, getting enraptured in the possibilities, ended by converting everything in sight to sexual membership (with the result that at one point in *The Castle* a wooden plank was copulating with an open window). This is the sort of excess Kafka inspires and it is, if anything, even more rampant in the Beckett criticism, especially that of *Godot*. And it has to do, obviously, with the peculiar stirrings that occur when "realism" and "symbolism" meet in powerfully mythic imaginations; that is, when an ontological parable is pulsating beneath a deceptive crust of actuality. Beckett's play, like Kafka's novels, would be unbearably boring were it not for the fact that its visible actuality, its text, is only a sham surface beneath which universal ideas are constantly generating, only to squirt away like tomato seeds under the finger of definition. We can say of *Godot* exactly what Roland Barthes says of Kafka's narrative: "[It] authorizes a thousand equally plausible keys—which is to say, it validates none."[8]

One of the most pervasive sources of this "mythic" effect is the play's way of speaking to us (or to no one) through its characters who, with one key exception I will discuss in the final chapter, are continually missing the point of their own conversation: they talk on the subject but have no idea what the subject is; they think they are waiting for a man named Godot or for night, literally, to fall. Even when a loaded, or intentional, image passes their lips it does so oxymoronically, with a profound triviality. For example:

Estragon: What about hanging ourselves?

          — — — — — — — — — — — —

  Pozzo: . . . . What is your name?
Estragon: Adam.

          — — — — — — — — — — — —

  Pozzo: . . . . Of the same species as Pozzo!
             Made in God's image![9]

Or, to take a more substantial passage which will serve as a locus of overall style:

Vladimir: I tell you his name is Pozzo.
Estragon: We'll soon see. *(He reflects.)* Abel! Abel!
  Pozzo: Help!
Estragon: Got it in one!
Vladimir: I begin to weary of this motif.
Estragon: Perhaps the other is called Cain. Cain! Cain!
  Pozzo: Help!

8. Roland Barthes, *Critical Essays*, trans. Richard Howard (Evanston, Ill.: Northwestern University Press, 1972), p. 136.
9. I am using the Grove Press edition throughout.

Estragon:	He's all humanity. *(Silence.)* Look at the little cloud.
Vladimir:	*(raising his eyes)* Where?
Estragon:	There. In the zenith.
Vladimir:	Well? *(Pause.)* What is there so wonderful about it?
	Silence.
Estragon:	Let's pass on now to something else, do you mind?

Here the play is suddenly astir with mythical depth. As through one of those perspective windows in a Renaissance painting, an ancient scene arises. But it is swallowed, just as suddenly, in what the play advertises as its subject: the boredom of waiting. If we examine this boredom from the standpoint of the play's deeper strategy, however, we see that it is a disguise beneath which we detect the author making a half-hearted escape, as if having gone too far toward being explicit ("accidentally on purpose"), he over-reacts and trivializes his image, literally, in this case, clouding it over. All in all, it is much the same tactic Iago uses on Othello: plant the truth by casually naming it, then urgently taking it back.

The question is, What truth, exactly, has been planted? Obviously, in this play, Abel and Cain are images of a very high priority. The trouble is, they come and go so fast that they can only be treated in slow motion, and it is precisely the speed of their passing that produces the hide-and-seek effect. As a contrast, think of the leisurely "classical" scene in which Hamlet picks up the skull in the graveyard and imagines it, among other things, to be "Cain's jawbone, that did the first murder." The keynote of this style, here as everywhere in Shakespeare, is in the forth-rightness and precision of focus. The idea is marching openly on the surface of the text and there is no doubt about what is meant: what more apt example of "all humanity" en route to the grave than that of the first murderer mortified? There is no contrivance, no obliquity; or rather, the contrivance is laid bare as a conflation of author and character. Though Shake-speare cannot be identified editorially with Hamlet, there is a sense in which his own intentions come snugly to rest in Hamlet's eloquence. Quite naturally, the play has given birth to this skull through the urgency of its own pregnancy with death; and quite naturally Hamlet elaborates its meanings. Our think-ing, you might say, is done for us and we are free to admire the thought.[10]

10. Here we have a reason why Shakespeare's symbols never be-come boring in their obviousness: his loading, or rather reloading, of the symbol (skull, sceptre, crown, flower, etc.) is principally a means of fortifying his theme with a catalogue of correspondences. It is not really the making of a symbol but the creation of a world perceived *through* the symbol. In the case above, the skull is actually an excuse to let in, as Macbeth's Porter puts it, "some of all profes-sions" unknowingly living life as if it would go on forever. Shake-speare begins with what amounts to a cliché and particularizes it, working backward from symbol to the experience out of which it has been formed. The modern playwright seems to proceed in the opposite direction. One of the risks he runs is that his symbols will be too explicit or commonplace. Hence he either disguises or buries his symbol, or titles his play after it, putting it out in the open as the play's given and then making the play itself a discourse on what the title means. Behind titles like *The Wild Duck, The Cherry Orchard,* or *The Glass Menagerie* we glimpse the modern writer

What is altogether absent in the Cain scene from *Godot* is just this forthright point of intellection; there is no *processing* consciousness which gives to the text a final authority.[11] Cain and Abel appear only latently, the code words of a certain rich history involving (if we pause to explicate) all sorts of thematic "shapes" relevant to the play: ownership of land, inhumanity, divine preferment and punishment, exile, wandering over the land, God's vengeful withdrawal from men's sight, etc. In short, there is a wave of unspecified meaning here and it produces, on its abrupt retreat, an undertow of the sort that one feels most powerfully in the presence of myth.

Actually, the mythic quality of this image has less to

exercising thematic control over his materials. Now and then, characters may have private interpretations of what the symbol means, but rarely does a single interpretation exhaust the implications. As a rule of thumb we could say that the more socially or politically oriented the playwright the clearer and more accessible his symbols are likely to be; the more metaphysically oriented, the more obscure. Obviously, this is not always the case, as we see in Kafka's *The Trial* which departs from a rather commonplace symbol toward the heady realms of abstract arrest and judgment. But, on balance, we might cite Pinter's version of the same dilemma, ironically titled *The Birthday Party*.

11. I would not make this claim for other Beckett plays like *Endgame* or *Krapp's Last Tape* in which there is a strong sense of a thinking mind brooding on the residue and meaning of experience. Characters like Hamm and Krapp "miss" very little, and anything cryptic or devious in their words seems to proceed from self-irony rather than ignorance. In fact, these plays may be thought of as extended recognition scenes or reports from the interior of a soul. *Godot* offers quite a different kind of subject matter, as my ensuing argument, I hope, will show.

do with the story of Abel and Cain than with something much less tangible. If we think about the image
for a moment, we see that it does not settle at all neatly
onto Pozzo or the Pozzo/Lucky situation (as, for
example, Cain becomes momentarily synonymous
with the skull in Hamlet's hand). The act of brother-
murder for which Cain and Abel are famous contains
far too much overkill to serve as a metaphor for Pozzo's victimization of Lucky, which we are invited to
associate with it. There is also the good possibility that
the image does not refer to Pozzo and Lucky at all, or
not only to them, but to Vladimir and Estragon who
are, in this scene, committing something of an outrage
on their fellowmen. In fact, earlier in this act there is
another oblique reference to Cain and Abel which does
exactly this and we should probably add it here since it
illustrates this same hide-and-seek tactic in reverse:

Estragon:	The best thing would be to kill me, like the other.
Vladimir:	What other? *(Pause.)* What other?
Estragon:	Like billions of others.
Vladimir:	*(sententious)* To every man his little cross. . . .

Here we have a clear case of fratricide but the criminal
escapes in the crowd. This "other" must certainly be
Cain (or Abel) in which case we should probably credit
Estragon with having an Adamic fixation, in addition
to his Christ complex. More to the point, however, is
why he should be so cryptic with Vladimir. In fact, the
image (if we can call it that) is virtually dragged into

this "simple" argument and carefully framed before being dropped. In other words, the master criminal here seems to be Beckett who steals his myth without actually naming it.

The point about such images is that they do not attach descriptively to characters or situations. Once out of a character's mouth they hover in the air of the play nonreferentially, the property of the play's idea. I don't mean to underrate the aptness of Beckett's images, but they are apt in a peculiar way. To illustrate: there is an old and rather Beckettesque joke about a factory employee who smuggled wheelbarrows past the night watchman by loading them with excelsior and hauling them right through the gate; that is, he deviated the watchman's attention from "the product" to its function, from the valuable to the valueless. Now the particulars of the Cain-Abel myth are far from valueless since, as we have seen, they form a strong constellation of latent meanings; but they do have a kind of excelsior-expendability which is reenforced, in part, by the throwaway tone. It is as if Cain and Abel had been chosen more for the fact of their fame than for the manner in which they earned it. In other words, they mask an even bigger theft and it is that of the entire Old Testament, that whole legendary Ur-world whose figures all possess in common a special family significance by virtue of their direct participation in the divine mystery. They are, in Erich Auerbach's phrase, "fraught with background," and it is this background, in all its priority and permanence, which is made momentarily visible in the figures of Abel and Cain, much as the violent history of the earth is made visible in a single outcropping of rock.[12]

All in all, the vast gulf between the trivial and the profound levels of meaning in the play offers an interpretive summons that is almost identical in principle to the figural interpretation of the Scriptures. That is, a *figura* is a "deceptive form" of something else. "The relation between the two events"—I quote now from Auerbach's essay, *"Figura"*—"is revealed by an accord or similarity. . . . Often vague similarities in the structure of events or in their attendant circumstances suffice to make the *figura* recognizable."[13] (Thus Adam is a *figura* of Christ, the Edenic tree a *figura* of the Cross, etc.) All this proceeds from the figural notion

12. This is not to discount the possibility that there are other, nonbiblical implications in Beckett's use of the Cain/Abel myth. For instance, John Pilling (*Samuel Beckett,* [London: Routledge & Kegan Paul, 1976]) notes that the image crops up often in Beckett's work and that "Every conception and every birth are a repetition and parody of the first conception and birth, which was the double birth of Cain and Abel from the coupling of Satan and Eve" (p. 119). I am concerned here, however, only with the sense in which the myth helps to conjure the spiritual "background" of the play. Along this line, I might note a further theological symbolism of Cain and Abel, which Beckett may or may not have had distantly in mind. For Augustine, Cain and Abel were central figures in the drama of God's graciousness, in which the two thieves are comparative newcomers. Cain is the founder of the City of Earth, Abel the founder of the City of God. Cain is the principle of sin ("the archetype of crime"), the "diabolical envious hatred with which the evil regard the good"; Abel is the principle of the "spiritual" and of all that God loved. First the carnal; then the spiritual. (See *The City of God,* trans. Marcus Dodo [New York: Random House, 1950], p. 482.

13. Erich Auerbach, *Scenes from the Drama of European Literature: Six Essays* (New York: Meridian Books, 1959), p. 29.

that God knows "no difference in time" (to quote Augustine) and therefore everything in the spiritual history of man—from God's point of view anyway—happens "concurrently simultaneously" (to quote Lucky). What I mean in applying this principle to *Godot* is that the play, on its most profound, or theological, level, depicts a further stage of the dilemma of "waiting" that originates with the Expulsion, is passed up through Adam's children in countless stories and parables which, as Auerbach says, are "enacted according to an ideal model which is a prototype situated in the future" (p. 59).

With this biblical world established, virtually from the title forward, as the play's "background" and kept intermittently in the picture by casual (or not so casual) hints, almost anything in it with sufficient "accord or similarity" is open to a figural interpretation. For example, a passage (cited by Auerbach) from Lactantius's third-century *Divinae institutiones* is tailormade as an account of how a day in the life of Vladimir and Estragon may be seen as a *figura* of human history:

We have frequently said that small and trivial things are figures and foreshadowings of great things; thus, this day of ours, which is bounded by sunrise and sunset, bears the likeness of that great day which is circumscribed by the passing of a thousand years. In the same way the *figuratio* of man on earth carried with it a parable of the heavenly people yet to be (p. 35).

Obviously we do not have to resort to figural methodology to reach the conclusion that Vladimir and Estragon stand for "all humanity," and it is

equally possible to interpret the play's "day" in a totally secular way: that is, as a *"figuratio"* of man on
earth bereft of a God or the remotest possibility of a
"heavenly" future. The idea is to show how readily the
play's "trivia" will foreshadow "great things" (which
are, have been, or will be) if one simply brings them
into its vicinity. As a more specific instance of how
such "things" inhere in the action, take the little scene
in which Vladimir and Estragon "do the tree":

Estragon: The tree?
              Vladimir does the tree, staggering about on one leg.
Vladimir: *(stopping)* Your turn.
              Estragon does the tree, staggers.
Estragon: Do you think God sees me?
Vladimir: You must close your eyes.
              Estragon closes his eyes, staggers worse.
Estragon: *(stopping, brandishing his fists, at the top of his
              voice).* God have pity on me!
Vladimir: *(vexed).* And me?
Estragon: On me! On me! Pity! On me!
              Enter Pozzo and Lucky, etc.

Ruby Cohn has suggested that this is a rendition of
exercise 52 in the Yoga series,[14] and it is quite possible
that Beckett had this in mind. But in terms of the play's
Christian symbolism, the scene would be better titled

14. "'Doing the tree' of *Godot* is exercise 52 in yoga series,
standing on one leg to pray, but Gogo cannot keep his balance, and
there is no evidence that God sees him" (*Back to Beckett*, [Princeton,
N.J.: Princeton University Press, 1973], p. 135). Others have made
the point that this scene resembles a crucifixion. For example:
Colin Duckworth, *En attendant Godot* (London: Harrap, 1966),
p. lix.

"doing the Cross." Here, under the guise of having the characters do exercises "for the balance," the play has them unknowingly act out the episode from which their key scriptural identity derives. It might be argued that this is reading into the play with a vengeance, but if the scene succeeds at all there must be "greater" implications of some sort, since there can be no conceivable interest in two men improving their motor skills late in Act II. And there are at least two "vague similarities" in the shape of this event which authorize the connection with the Cross: the first is the very posture that is suggested by "doing" the tree; the other is the direct address to God which recalls the thief's plea to Christ for mercy. (As documented in *Luke:* "Lord, remember me when thou comest into thy kingdom." The other thief says, "If thou be Christ, save thyself and us.") We can deduce little beyond this (for example, which character is which thief); nor can the identity of the two thieves be strictly equated with Vladimir and Estragon who are simply the play's primary "carriers" of what we might call the two-thieves principle, or the paradox (as Beckett sees it at least) of grace unaccountably given and unaccountably withheld.[15] In fact, the deepest resonances of the Cain/Abel image rest precisely in their being the first

15. I'm sure someone has already noticed this, but I've wondered if there isn't a possible connection between Didi and Gogo and Dysmas and Gestas, the names given to the two thieves in the Middle Ages (see the apocryphal *Acts of Pilate*), especially if one recalls that Beckett is the man who gave us a certain Mr. Obidil (libido) in the trilogy. It would be an interesting point for a director to bear in mind for an audience with theological scruples, particularly in the placement of the two men in the second "Crucifixion" scene.

figuratio of this principle. All this is hopelessly dis-
torted, but if it were made much clearer the scene
would not succeed, except perhaps as low comedy,
and an actor (or scene designer) would be well advised
not to emphasize anything "crosslike" in the pro-
ceedings; for one would violate the play to comment
openly on what it had taken pains to keep implicit.

In fact, we might view Beckett's whole stylistic
problem in *Godot* from just this angle: how to keep this
background—which is one term of the play's vast
spiritual metaphor—*in* the background, out of the
foreground where it would certainly begin dictating
terms and reducing the argument of the play to that of
an allegory, however dark and perverse, on the order
of *Everyman* or *The Castle of Perseverance*. For it is clear:
this play cannot afford to exploit its spiritual content
too openly (to call God God) or it runs the serious risk

Dysmas (crucified to Christ's right) was the repentant thief. He
entered heaven with a cross on his shoulders, the first mortal re-
deemed by Christ's death. But which tramp should have the
honor? Didi seems the logical beneficiary, given his preoccupation
with repentance and crucifixion throughout the play; and at the
end he does speak the words, "Christ have mercy upon us." Unfortunately, this would consign Gogo to a fate worse than death
and that is hardly what the play has in mind. But if the reader finds
this idea far-fetched, consider one propounded by Beckett himself
on Estragon's chances: "One of Estragon's feet is blessed, and the
other damned. The boot won't go on the foot that is damned; and it
will go on the foot that is not. It is like the two thieves on the cross"
(Harold Hobson, "Samuel Beckett," [see note 1], p. 153). I simply
don't know what to make of this: it seems to be carrying thievery
to the limit of subtlety (Should one presume, or despair?). Perhaps
we should call it a stand-off: Estragon gets at least one foot in the
gate, which is more than we can clearly say for Vladimir.

of being swamped by heavy ideas, on one hand, or becoming maudlin with concern for man, on the other. To put the question more positively: How (on the theory that form, to some extent, should follow function) can the play maintain an aesthetic distance from its true subject (man after the Fall) which might approximate its audience's spiritual distance from the Promise held forth "in the beginning"? Or, as Beckett once put it: How "to find a form which accommodates the mess?"[16]

I think Beckett solved this problem, with the homing instinct of a true eschatologist, by adapting certain qualities of biblical style. The qualities I have in mind are conveniently summarized by Auerbach in *Mimesis*: "certain parts [of the text] brought into high relief, others left obscure, abruptness, suggestive influence of the unexpressed, 'background' quality, multiplicity of meanings and the need for interpretation, universal-historical claims, development of the concept of the historically becoming, and preoccupation with the problematic."[17] Most of these features would probably apply to many modern works which have nothing to do with the Bible or with religious matters; but with respect to mythic "linguistics," as distinct from myth content, the list seems an especially good catalogue of the stylistic features of *Godot*. In other words, *Godot* is not (like MacLeish's *J.B.* or Giraudoux's *Judith*) an old

16. In Tom F. Driver, "Beckett by the Madeleine," *Columbia University Forum* 4, No. 3 (Summer 1961): 23.
17. Erich Auerbach, *Mimesis: The Representation of Reality in Western Literature,* trans. Willard R. Trask (Princeton, N.J.: Princeton University Press, 1953), p. 23.

biblical myth in modern dress but a new myth, or
story about the plight of modern man, in old dress; it is
a parable for today, such as might appear in a latter-day
Bible aimed at accommodating modern problems of
despair and alienation. Moreover, Beckett has further
observed the canons of biblical style in choosing his
parable from humble life (two tramps holding the
Christian vigil, as opposed to two kings or phi-
losophers); thus, as Auerbach says, he connects the
lowest and the highest, *humilitas* and *sublimitas,* so that
while speaking simply, as if to children, the text of the
play opens "secrets and riddles which are revealed to
very few" (p. 134). Again, this may not be unusual in
our era of common-man realism, but it helps to account for *Godot's* unique double appeal: unlike *Endgame* or *Happy Days*—unlike any serious play I can
name, in fact—it can be enjoyed as a clown show by
children who have no historical or doctrinal memory
to interfere with its clowning; and, it goes without
saying, critics and theologians are still searching its
secrets and riddles with a seemingly endless capacity
for Adoration of the Text.

Unfortunately, this description of biblical or "mythic" style suggests that we are dealing with some sort of
portable device (like the sonnet form or iambic pen-
tameter) which can be put out on loan. It is not really a
style, as such, that I am trying to pin down here but a
form of linguistic energy, apparently timeless, which
occurs in various degrees of intensity and combination
with other forms of energy. When the "charge" is
strong enough, it tends to attract the word *mythic,* with
or without the approval of anthropology or the dictio-

nary. Like the Sublime, myth is a slippery customer open to all sorts of metaphorical violation; but one is struck by the fact that discussions of myth, or more correctly of the mythic effect, seem to turn eventually on a "background" quality which is not necessarily traceable to an ancestral content originating back in the seasonal mists. Casual usages of the words *myth* and *mythic* imply an arousing of what Yeats called "the emotion of multitude."[18] William Empson says that double plots "work on you like a myth,"[19] the idea being that when there are two or more versions of something (the Lear/Gloucester plots, for example), you have the sense of the example disappearing in the precept, or the copy in the archetype.[20] Narrative content is subdued by the rigor of a pattern that appears by fiat of an absent hand and exists, as Alfred N. Whitehead says, in virtue of "the doom of [its] realization. . . . And this doom consigns the pattern to play its part in an uprush of feeling, which is the awakening of infinitude to finite activity."[21]

Pattern of course is not myth; but we cannot go far into myth without encountering the principle of pattern, or repetition-compulsiveness (the serial adventures of an individual myth, the migration of a myth to new contents, etc.). Something like this seems to be

18. William Butler Yeats, *Essays and Introductions* (New York: Macmillan, 1961), pp. 215–216.
19. William Empson, *English Pastoral Poetry* (New York: Norton, 1938), p. 54.
20. The latter phrase is Auerbach's: *"Figura,"* in *Scenes from the Drama,* p. 49.
21. Alfred N. Whitehead, *A Philosopher Looks at Science* (New York: Philosophical Library, 1965), p. 23.

behind Levi-Strauss's insistence that a myth consists of all its versions: Freud's version of the Oedipus myth, he says, is just as "authentic" as Sophocles'. So is Seneca's or Voltaire's or Cocteau's. But in any single play or fiction based conspicuously on the Oedipus story, this background quality is likely to be lost, or at least diminished, because the work is simply a new version of what was already (in Sophocles' play) a literary displacement of "the original." It is Oedipus the King who is being imitated, not the intuitive perception which at some lost point in time led to Oedipus. Thus the myth ceases to be a "thinking of the body" and becomes a host for relevant civic discourse. Thebes becomes the scene of a critical cultural issue, just as Argos in Sartre's *The Flies,* becomes the locale in which the problem of Existential freedom is to be examined. Precisely what falls away in these updatings of myth is the background (now in the foreground), the intuitive perception which was expressible only by symbolic concealment, only by calling it what it was not. As such, the literary version of the myth bears the same relation to its "original" content as the psychiatrist's interpretation does to the patient's dream.

In his discussion of the mythical in the Socratic dialogues, Kierkegaard remarks that the age of myth is already past as soon as the question of a mythical representation arises: "As long as the myth is taken for actuality it is not properly myth."[22] My interest here has

22. Søren Kierkegaard, *The Concept of Irony, with Constant Reference to Socrates,* trans. Lee M. Capel (Bloomington: Indiana University Press, 1968), p. 133. An interesting variation of this same idea is offered by Schopenhauer: "A religion . . . has only the obligation to be true *sensu allegorico,* since it is destined for the innumer-

little to do with what myths actually are, or may be, but with the way a text can behave mythically, or work on us *like* a myth. It seems to me that it does not have only to do with the presence of a myth-content in the text (the Oedipus story, Christ and the thieves, Adam and the Fall, Cain and Abel) but with a particular way in which the text clothes its myth and controls the reader's participation.

On this elusive ground no one is better than Kierkegaard, and since this concept of the mythical is central here I would like to pursue his distinction between myth and the mythical. "It seems superfluous," he says,

to call attention to the fact that one cannot call [a Platonic dialogue] mythical simply because it contains a reference to some myth, for referring to a myth does not make a representation mythical; nor is it mythical because it uses a myth,

---

able multitude who, being incapable of investigating and thinking, would never grasp the profoundest and most difficult truths *sensu proprio*. Before the people truth cannot appear naked. A symptom of this *allegorical* nature of religions is the *mysteries*, to be found perhaps in every religion, that is, certain dogmas that cannot even be distinctly conceived, much less be literally true. In fact, it might perhaps be asserted that some absolute inconsistencies and contradictions, some actual absurdities, are an essential ingredient of a complete religion; for these are just the stamp of its *allegorical* nature, and the only suitable way of making the ordinary mind and uncultured understanding *feel* what would be incomprehensible to it, namely that religion deals at bottom with an entirely different order of things, an order of *things-in-themselves*. In the presence of such an order the laws of this phenomenal world, according to which it must speak, disappear"(*The World as Will and Representation*, II, trans. E. F. J. Payne [New York: Dover Publications, 1966], p. 166).

for this clearly shows one is above it; nor is a representation mythical because one seeks to transform a myth into an object of belief, for the mythical is not addressed primarily to the understanding but to the imagination. The mythical requires that the individual abandon himself to this, and only when the representation oscillates in this way between the production and reproduction of the imagination is the representation mythical.[23]

The example Kierkegaard gives is Diotima's narrative of Eros's birth in the *Symposium*. It is not, however, the allusion to Eros, as a mythical character, which constitutes the mythical interest in the dialogue, but the fact that the tale of his parentage—he is the offspring of Poros (Plenty) and Penia (Penury)—allows the Idea (the paradoxical nature of love) to be "seen." In This case, the Idea, which Socrates has to this point been pursuing dialectically, is that love is a mean between wisdom and ignorance, fairness and foulness, good and evil, the divine and the mortal. Through the myth of Eros, this abstraction is actualized and maintained in the time and space of a wholly "imaginary reality"; the Idea is "placed outside thought and entrusted to imagination" (p. 139). The myth is "the Idea in a condition of estrangement, its externality, . . . its immediate temporality and spaciality as such" (p. 132).

Many critics would probably find this concept of the mythical far too fanciful to be of use to the anthropological study of myth. I cite it here because it illustrates, as well as anything in myth criticism I have

23. *The Concept of Irony,* pp. 136–137.

read, the fundamentally creative nature of myth-seeing—that mystery or "uprush of feeling" that takes place when you suddenly, or gradually, perceive that the text you are reading is in some devious or hidden sense "oscillating" (as Kierkegaard says) with something else, being in effect foreordained, though the point of ordination is nowhere to be seen. It does not have to be a bona fide myth that is informing the fiction; any recognizable model will serve. For example, the fiction may have generated its own "myth," as Molloy's Easter journey is iterated by Moran's journey, or more obviously as Act I of *Godot* becomes the myth of which Act II is a new version. This process of oscillation is perhaps the most compelling sense in which a reader participates in the creation, or completion, of the Idea a text is generating (the perception of an object or a person as a symbol is a narrower version of the same process), and it goes without saying that it is also the source of a great deal of textual abuse in myth criticism.[24]

By creative, of course, I do not mean that the reader actually creates anything; I mean simply that there is a freedom of inference, passed over to the reader. Half the text, you might say, exists only in him, in his memory; he must "finish" the text on his own, somewhat as children draw a picture in an exercise book by sequentially connecting the numbered dots with

24. An excellent recent treatment of the creative nature of myth-seeing and the abuses it inspires in modern criticism is William Righter's *Myth and Literature* (London and Boston: Routledge & Kegan Paul, 1975).

straight lines, or as one might "hear" the whole of a familiar song, played at a distance, in intermittent notes that reach the ear.

This may be a metaphoric corruption of the word *mythical,* but it perhaps describes the ground of attraction that certain texts have for readers. One detects and tracks myth in a literary text by undergoing what amounts to a division of mind. As Kierkegaard says, the mythical is not addressed primarily to the understanding but to the imagination. It is "the enthusiasm of the imagination in the service of speculation" (p. 132). Of course, he is speaking here of myth as it works reciprocally with dialectic in the Platonic dialogues, but the same process may occur in nonspeculative experience as well. For example, there is a passage in Beckett's *Proust* that strikes me as being as good an explanation of Kierkegaard's concept of the mythical in Plato as it is of the Proustian remembrance of things past:

The identification of immediate with past experience, the recurrence of past action or reaction in the present, amounts to a participation between the ideal and the real, imagination and direct apprehension, symbol and substance. Such participation frees the essential reality that is denied to the contemplative as to the active life. What is common to present and past is more essential than either taken separately. Reality, whether approached imaginatively or empirically remains a surface, hermetic. Imagination, applied—a priori—to what is absent, is exercised in vacuo and cannot tolerate the limits of the real. Nor is any direct and purely experimental contact possible between subject and object, because they are automatically separated by the subject's consciousness of perception, and the object loses its purity and becomes a mere intellectual pretext or motive. But, thanks to this reduplication, the experience is at once imaginative and empirical, at once an evocation and direct perception, real without being merely actual, ideal without being merely abstract, the ideal real, the essential, the extratemporal. But if this mystical experience communicates an extratemporal essence, it follows that the communicant is for the moment an extratemporal being.[25]

Although the word Beckett uses here is "mystical," the experience is what one might call the "personal mythical," the sense in which one relives one's own private archetypes.

This is perhaps enough to communicate the sense in which I am using the concept of the mythical. But by way of stretching the implications a step further I would cite one more text that introduces a modern variation of the background principle. I refer to Roland Barthes' *Mythologies,* a book that deals not with the recurrence of old myths but with the manner in which certain phenomena of modern culture (ornamental cookery, guide-books, plastic, etc.) become mythologized. Myth is conceived by Barthes as a language, or a form, which may attach itself to anything. Myth is speech *"stolen and restored.* Only, speech which is restored is no longer quite that which was stolen: when it was brought back, it was not put exactly in its place. It is this brief act of larceny, this moment taken

25. *Proust,* pp. 55–56.

for a surreptitious faking, which gives mythical speech its benumbed look."[26] One of the central characteristics of myth (to ignore a great deal else in this complex essay) is that is reproduces "the physique of the alibi"; it always has "an elsewhere" at its disposal: "I am not where you think I am: I am where you think I am not" (p. 123).

Godot would not at all qualify as a myth in Barthes' definition (see, for example, his discussion of contemporary poetry as a "regressive" language which "resists myth as much as it can," p. 133); the idea I want to recover here is that his "elsewhere" and Auerbach's "background"—secular and religious variations, respectively, of the same principle—seem to me to over-

---

26. *Mythologies,* trans. Annette Lavers (New York: Hill and Wang, n.d.), p. 125. Barthes' book is filled with examples of how the language of myth is used in modern culture. Perhaps the one that will illustrate the point most succinctly is that of the *Paris-Match* cover on which a Negro soldier is saluting the French tricolor. Here the "drive behind the myth" is to proclaim the concept of French imperiality, the zeal of French patriotism, by appropriating the Negro and condemning him to be "nothing more than an instrumental signifier," *"one of our own boys"* (pp.124–125). This use of myth is obviously the soul of advertising which "steals" myths and their signifiers from other languages and puts them in fresh, and usually irrelevant, commercial contexts to sell products (for example, the myth of the clean healthy outdoor life as signified by the rugged cowboy in the Marlboro ad). In this sense of myth, it would be difficult to exhaust the mythological content of any play, since all plays are bound by a culture and its ring of myths. The impressive thing about *Godot* is that it appropriates so many myths as part of its tension. To give but one example that would perhaps satisfy Barthes' concept of myth: is not the very absence of a thickening plot (which the play frequently alludes to) a source of tension through which the play's own static plot, on one level at least, becomes a conflict between traditional dramatic practice (what plays are supposed to do, so to speak, for a living) and the demand

lap on substantially the same linguistic goings-on that we find in *Godot*. That is, the play derives a mythic tension from the constant "oscillation" of background and foreground, elsewhere and here, a coming in and out of focus of what are often contradictory loadings of the same shape, much in the manner of that old trick drawing of Jastrow's which is, by turns, a rabbit and a duck.[27] The reading of the play (less so, presumably, seeing it on stage) is thus a constant effort at translation: trivial to profound, comic to serious, temporal to essential, etc., and vice versa. This is not properly an act of translation (except among critics) but an interrupted movement toward, an instability which may be

---

for new freedoms, surfacing after the war? One has the impression that lines like "This is becoming really insignificant" are half spoken to the audience on a dare: "This isn't what you expect in 'good' theatre, is it?" Of course, now that *Godot* is thoroughly our play this tension has been set to rest. But in the fifties it was the Messiah of what Poggioli calls "the religion of liberty"; since then it has itself become mythologized in hundreds of plays in which one sees the Holy Ghost of its victory over plot translated into boredom of a different sort.

27. The idea of contradictory meanings and paradoxes in Beckett's work is scarcely a new one. For example, see E. M. Scarry, "Six Ways To Kill a Blackbird or Any Other Intentional Object: Samuel Beckett's Method of Meaning," *James Joyce Quarterly* 8, No. 4 (Summer 1971): 278–289; Stanley E. Gray, "Beckett and Queneau as Formalists," *James Joyce Quarterly* 8, No. 4 (Summer 1971): 392–404; Francis Doherty, *Samuel Beckett* (London: Hutchinson University Library, 1971), esp. p. 89ff; David H. Hesla, *The Shape of Chaos: An Interpretation of the Art of Samuel Beckett* (Minneapolis: University of Minnesota Press, 1971). It is almost unnecessary, in connection with this theme, to add the names of Hugh Kenner (*Samuel Beckett,* see note 7), and Vivian Mercier whose most recent book (*Beckett/Beckett,* see note 7), is devoted exclusively to oppositions and levels of dialectic in Beckett's work.

likened to a mild though aesthetically absorbing frustration at the synapse.

This frustration, or creative activity, is continuous
in one's reading of the play; it does not well up only in
the presence of significant images like Cain and Abel. I
can illustrate this on the very lowest verbal level by
returning to the image of the cloud in the Cain/Abel
passage. If any image in the play carries a near-zero
charge it is surely this one. Yet even here, precisely
because the image is such a sudden low-pressure
"hole" in the excitement, is an instance in which the
urge to translate might have trouble escaping its own
momentum. What is the cloud doing up there so
gratuitously, so ostentatiously "wonderful"? Might it
be something more, as Hamlet would have it, a *whale*
of a cloud? There is, of course, the good chance that it is
simply a cloud, nothing more; but once framed in the
attention, possibilities arise; it might, for example, represent nature passing indifferently over "all humanity," like the cloud the wounded Prince Andrey sees
going its peaceful pantheistic way over the battlefield
at Austerlitz (the situation in progress would certainly
support such a reading); or, could it be a cloud with
quite a different, and more relevant, kind of god in it,
as in those passages in the Bible where God appears in
the form of a cloud.[28] The point is not what one can

28. For example: "While he yet spake, behold, a bright cloud over-
shadowed them: and behold a voice out of the cloud, which said,
This is my beloved Son. . ." (Matthew 17:5; or "I saw in the
night visions, and, behold, one like the Son of man came with the
clouds of heaven. . ." (Daniel 7:13). The idea, to be discussed in
Chapter 3, is that Godot, or a sign from him, may possibly have
arrived in this scene.

make of the image but that such pockets of emptiness
are never reliably insignificant (a word this play flau-
nts). All this, of course, would scarcely be the case in
more realistic fiction where descriptive demands alone
guarantee a certain hypertrophy of imagery, purely in
the interests of filling out the scene. But in a text so
spare, so cunningly random, everything is a lure. Well
and good for Beckett to insist there are no symbols
where none are intended, but he himself (like a boy
who failed to cry wolf) has set the conditions whereby
all images, the more off-handed the more suspicious,
loom as potential motifs in the grand design.

II
Generic Time and Place

It is often said that Beckett gives us generic landscapes and situations: his plays take place in hypothetical time and space. But how does a play go about creating this effect? What is it about *Godot,* in stylistic terms, that makes us resort to this word *generic* and its synonyms (universal, archetypal, etc.) so often?

Clearly a play does not achieve this effect by calling for a locale we recognize because we have seen it "elsewhere." One suspects that it has something to do with purity of design, the sense of a clear unchanging shape emerging from all the detail—as in certain paintings one can readily detect the pure geometric "archetypes" of all paintings (circle, square, triangle) emerging from the representation. In short, is it not possible to make almost anything generic by reducing it far enough, to one overwhelming attribute? Detail obscures form. And to the extent that sociological milieu, say, stands in the way of a play's design we would be less likely to call it generic or archetypal: the play has been bogged down in punctual matters, which is to say in the effect of a unique set of cultural conditions on a unique set of people.

I am thinking here mainly of one's overall or first impressions. For instance, in the plays of Ibsen, the master of sociological milieu, there are plenty of archetypes and mythic signals. But one must uncover them by squinting out the continuous procession of representative details in which the archetype is hidden. (It is interesting to note, in fact, that Ibsen criticism has only recently begun to see these archetypes, having been long preoccupied with the busy sociological "surface" of his plays.) The intermediary between Ibsen and Beckett is Chekhov, whose world is just as crowded with paraphernalia as Ibsen's. But there is a *plus ça change* principle at work in Chekhov through which his obsessive archetype of dispossession is constantly asserting itself. Things do not become more complex, only more so. What Chekhov and Beckett share is a psychology of plot we might call Enigma Variations and the "elsewhere" that lures us is often simply the ghost of one of the play's own earlier parts.[1]

"That which gives space reality," Kierkegaard says, "is the organic process of nature, that which gives time reality is the content of history."[2] Thus realism—that

1. Realism since Chekhov and Maeterlinck describes a growing fascination with the *plus ça change* principle: the event is crowded out by its own psychological interstices. One of the purest recent examples is David Storey's *The Changing Room* in which the winning or losing of a football game is totally incidental to the pre-, mid-, and post-game life of the players as expressed in the business of changing from "street" clothing to game uniform and back again. In short, everything that a playwright might have made drama of before Beckett (including the personal lives and domestic conflicts of the players) is kept off-stage while the play scrupulously examines the behavior of men trapped in the weekly round of playing the game. The act of putting on a uniform, or "changing," is an act of not changing at all, of submission to a deadening habit which sums up the characters' lives.
2. *The Concept of Irony,* trans. Lee M. Capel (Bloomington: Indiana University Press, 1968), p. 137n.

facade, Beckett says in *Proust,* behind which the Idea is prisoner[3]—would be an attempt to depict a scene that has grown out of a specific organic process of nature; its here-and-now aspect is nothing but the visible process of a history working its way out. In this sense, description, even in historical novels about long-ago-and-far-away events, is an elaborate process of littering, or embedding space in real time. You can destroy the generic effect of Beckett's wasteland ("A country road. A tree. Evening."), or at least set it at odds with the action it is to contain, by simply littering it with the content of a history (refuse, ruins, billboards), things heavy with a definite past and consequently destined for future use. Chekhov's famous remark that if there is a pistol on stage in Act I it must be fired in Act IV is a condensation of this idea: objects in the dramatic universe are "waiting" objects; like traps, they exist only to exert their potential.

Over against realism we would place the mythical representation in which, as Kierkegaard goes on to say, "both time and space have only imaginary reality" (p. 137n). For example, when the Indian myth tells us that a king reigned 70,000 years, it uses a specific determination of time but deprives it of "validity" by "squandering" it. This principle of squandering time, and space, offers a useful way into the problem, for *Godot* spends a good deal of its time doing just that. I am not referring to squandering in the sense of characters wasting, or killing time, but of ways in which the play itself avoids entrapment in clock time and finite space.[4]

3. *Proust,* (New York: Grove Press, n.d.), p. 59.
4. Readers who may find Kierkegaard's concept of mythical representation unique or idiosyncratic will find a more recent corrob-

Being a fiction, and specifically a tragicomic one, *Godot* can not afford to be so openly imaginary as the Indian myth, but as a simple instance of the squandering of time, take the line, "We should have thought of it a million years ago, in the nineties." This is a kind of joke, or insinuation of a racial past for these two men in the same equivocal vein as the title itself, which gives God his extratemporal reality with one syllable and winks at it with the other. Still, in the context of a play so titled, do we not take the phrase "a million years ago" as a hint that more is meant here than the cliché for "long ago" (last year, thirty years ago)? It implies the same refusal to come to rest in a specific history as the refusal of the play's tree (a squandered space) to abide by the laws of botanical growth. Or, again, when Estragon says, "But what Saturday? And is it Saturday? Is it not rather Sunday? *(Pause.)* Or Monday? *(Pause)* Or Friday?" he is squandering time, putting the play outside all temporal reality while seeming to be immersed in its categories. It could be argued that this is a simple act of forgetting (as when they forget where they were to meet Godot: "You're sure it was here?"); but the failure of memory in Beckett, apart from what it contributes to the fugitive quality of life in his world, is also a built-in convenience by which the play is able to escape all moorings in time and space that might lock the characters into a causal history (as such moorings do to Ibsen's characters—who have excellent memories).

---

oration in Wilbur M. Urban's chapter on "Religion and The Mythical Consciousness" in *Humanity and Deity* (London: Allen and Unwin, 1951), particularly pp. 98–99.

The play is, in fact, one continuous escape from the primacy of substance and almost any detail will illustrate the point. Take, for instance, the fact that Estragon is beaten every night. Here is evidence that the world out there is, as Shakespeare's Benedick would say, "peopled." And there is a fair nearby where Pozzo hopes to sell Lucky for "a good price." How, precisely, do these things exist? Certainly not in the palpable way that the offstage world exists in Ibsen, or in the overcrowded cities of Ionesco. There is something suspiciously improbable, anachronistic, about these signs of life in the environs of Godot-land. What sort of thugs, or fair, can we conjure in the mind's eye that are not immediately "invalidated" by the nothingness of the landscape ("Recognize! What is there to recognize?")? Pozzo never reaches the fair, Estragon shows no bruises, or at least the play makes nothing of these possibilities. These events exist nebulously, to quote Barthes "the condensation, more or less hazy, of a certain knowledge"[5]—the knowledge here being that of *all* violence, *all* commerce.

So too with the proper names in the play, of which there are more than we normally find in Ibsen or Chekhov; the Eiffel Tower, the Rhone, the Pyrenees, Kapp and Peterson, Fulham, Clapham, Cunard, Connemara, Bishop Berkeley, etc. Here a play would normally gather ballast in real time and space. But these names exist unreferentially, as if they had been chosen for their sound alone; they are the interchangable artifacts of a formerly real world, or a real *other*

5. *Mythologies,* trans. Annette Lavers (New York: Hill and Wang, n.d.), p. 122.

world.[6] Other names would have served as well, as, for example, Estragon's Catulle in the French version was eventually changed to Adam in the English. Adam may be an improvement, a more universal image than Catulle, as one critic has suggested [7] (Beckett's explanation: "We got fed up with Catullus"[8]), but it was an improvement that did not disturb the text: the text will tolerate change because its images rarely have a transitive life. The same might even be said (though less securely) of Cain and Abel: Jacob and Esau would probably have made as much sense, or at least would send us chasing in similar corridors of the same palace of victimage. Something, admittedly, would be lost, but something would be gained as well. The point is that what we can infer, after the fact, from Cain and Abel, or what we *might* infer from Jacob and Esau (the idea of stolen blessing) would be supported by the rest of the play because it is so docile, so amenable to adjustment: it will surround what food it is given, like an amoeba.[9]

Then there are the actual things *in* Beckett's world

6. The point is not contradicted by the fact that many of these names, like Joyce's names, may have particular meanings or an autobiographical status for Beckett.

7. Eugene Webb, *The Plays of Samuel Beckett* (Seattle: University of Washington Press, 1972), p. 144.

8. Colin Duckworth, *En attendant Godot,* (London: Harrap, 1966), pp. lxiii–lxiv.

9. I am not implying that the organization of the play is arbitrary or "amenable to adjustment," though in one sense it might be easier to shift some of the scenes of *Godot* than those, say, of Ibsen or Chekhov. Here, of course, I am dealing with formal and poetic matters of mood, rhythm, and overall "build," on which ground the words of *Godot* are, as we say, in "the best order" possible.

(boots, hats, radishes, rope, etc.) which serve to "naturalize" his world, to take the voices out of the void and provide such occasions for action and reaction as the world affords. In the second act, for example, there is the scene of the discovery of the boots which, as Estragon is quick to note, serve the wonderful purpose of giving them the impression that they exist. The scene consists of Vladimir's more or less successful attempt to get the boots on Estragon's feet, with the two of them wreathed together and staggering, three-footed, about the stage. Here we are literally in the thick of things, at the heart of the play's "realism." Yet what leaps out of this thickness is precisely an abstraction, or the impression that these boots and the human confrontation with them are but another embodiment of what was earlier being done with the hats and will later be done with a piece of rope. Like props on a magician's table, these things (common, innocuous) can be taken up consecutively, or in any order, and submitted to the same act of magical transformation. *Plus ça change.* Hugh Kenner, on the nature of objects in *Godot,* says that the play "contains no item owning a past, a future, or a duration with which our vital sentiment may feel empathy."[10] Converted to my thesis, this is to say that such objects have no integral part in an organic process of nature, in a history, and by this default they gain a kind of emphasis, or independence from any contingent role.

10. *Samuel Beckett: A Critical Study,* (Berkeley and Los Angeles: University of California Press, 1973), p. 151. See also: John D. Erickson, "Objects and Systems in the Novels of Samuel Beckett," *L'Esprit créateur* 7, No. 2 (Summer 1967): 113–122.

What lurks in them, primarily, is resistance, a passive conspiracy of the natural order against the human. It is as if the magician's props had a magical act of their own and could triumph, at will, over the magician's plan. It is said that Godot is named after the French slang for boot *(godillot)*. [11] This may be Beckett's way of setting to rest any divine pretensions of his title, but there is at least an unintentional truth in the notion that a god can be coterminous with an object. Augustine's idea that God is "most hidden and most near," present in all of his creation, is no less true here: in perfect self-consistency a Godot inheres in this scene in the laws of probability by which boots unaccountably appear (or may be the same ones left yesterday) and both fit and do not fit. Like the carafe and the scissors in *Act Without Words* they exist by virtue of their catalytic power to produce the fundamental frustration in the Beckett world.

We may also note that this scene is encased within the parentheses of two silences—silence, among its other functions, being the play's insurance that nothing will become promise-crammed and leak toward a future. To understand just how intransitive the scene is one has only to imagine it taking place in an Ibsen living room where physical action is limited to purposive movement ("Brack crosses to table.") and objects behave as the obedient extensions of the conflict in progress: Lovborg's manuscript conveniently con-

11. See Richard Gilman, "Beckett," *Partisan Review* 41, No. 1 (1974): 58. There are, of course, other associations one might make with the word "Godot." These are discussed by Colin Duckworth, pp. cxiii-cxvi.

sents to be lost, is found by the right person, and destroyed by a fire which was only incidentally set to keep the room warm. In Ibsen, as in most realism, the space and time in which the play unfolds is clearly marked by the progress of its objects, each of which is the visible token of a premise in the overall dialectic. This is also true of Chekhov: in the last act of *The Cherry Orchard* the furniture is covered with shrouds and there is a look of desolation in everything: this is the desolation of mind made visible, the shrouds cover the corpse of an idea, and by the sympathetic magic of the symbol we are made to see the ghost of an era in a vacant room.

As an almost obligatory instance of squandering on a big scale, I turn finally to Lucky's great speech which is not only the play's largest single structural unit but its most sustained reference to the real world of men and nature. Almost every critic has written about this speech and most of the commentary is devoted to isolating its thematic contribution. The usual view, which originates with Raymond Williams, is that it is a definition, in garbled syllogistic form, of the human predicament as the play itself acts it out: given the existence of a personal God, it is established beyond all doubt that man is plunged in torment, wastes and pines, the skull fading, fading.[12] And it ends in a corruption of Christ's last words on the cross which gives

12. I have abbreviated William's text which can be found in Alan Simpson's *Beckett and Behan And A Theatre in Dublin* (London: Routledge & Kegan Paul, 1962), p. 128, and in the Ruby Cohn *Casebook on Waiting for Godot* (New York: Grove Press, 1967), p. 49.

rise to the idea that Lucky, like Estragon, sees life as a perverted ongoing Crucifixion.

There is little doubt that the speech is spun out on some such bleak axis. What this view sacrifices, however, is the sheer pictorial density of its mass. What happens as the speech proceeds is that this frenzied attempt to "establish" a basic proposition, or certainty, about man in the world becomes hopelessly engulfed in the variety in which the world asserts itself. In short, the speech may be a parody of academic "thinking," but it is also a great verbal frieze, or the ruin of one, depicting a whole world bound on one side by the processes of life (labor, physical culture, alimentation, defecation, etc.) and on the other by the processes of nature. For all this, it is not a real world because it lacks connective tissue, contingency; but something like a logic emerges. In fact, the salient dramatic feature of the speech is that it simulates an explosion: as it builds, the human world of Fulham and Clapham gradually "fades" and is overwhelmed by a catastrophe that sounds suspiciously like the death of a star ("the rivers running water running fire . . . and then the earth in the great cold the great dark the air and the earth abode of stones in the great cold").[13] At the center one somehow sees a group of busy scholars laboring the big questions of God, man, and matter in the Academy; and outside, on the fields and lakes and

13. I am not the first critic to make this point. For example, see: Richard Coe, "God and Samuel Beckett," *Meanjin* 24 (1965): 72; John J. Sheedy, "The Net," *Casebook on Waiting for Godot,* p. 164; Ruby Cohn, *Back to Beckett* (Princeton, N.J.: Princeton University Press, 1973), p. 136.

lawns, the rest of humanity is making great strides in sports of all kinds; all this against the backdrop of the world of the elements churning away—in spite of the tennis—toward entropy or toward some sort of apocalypse. So we end with something like a rewriting of Montaigne's dictum: ". . . there is no constant existence, either of our own being, or of that of what we observe. Both we and our judgment and all mortal things are incessantly flowing and rolling on."[14]

All in all, it is an excellent example of a "containing" speech: it reaches out toward *essential* matters (man in Essy), the idea being that if a dramatist would examine man thoroughly, he must put him in some sort of a universe, not merely in a locale. And one might say that Beckett's main purpose in giving Lucky this speech, carefully "cured" in his long silence preceding it, was to expand the implications of waiting into final realms: tennis and thought in the context of the firmament. It is by a similar logic that Shakespeare has Hamlet, talking to Rosencrantz and Guildenstern about his ailment, deliver his great "What a piece of work is a man" speech which sets man, the quintessence of dust, against the brave o'erhanging firmament. And so on through Shakespeare: whenever there is an occasion to reverberate the spiritual qualm into the world at large, we get something like a Lucky speech (in principle at least)—Timon's "Each thing's a thief," Macbeth's "Tomorrow and tomorrow" or Ulysses' speech on the universal wolf. Or, finally, as a

14. "Apology for Raymond Sebond," *The Essays of Michel de Montaigne,* Vol. I, trans. George B. Ives (New York: Heritage Press, 1946), p. 812.

classical prototype of this same impulse to generalize, we might cite the chapter in *The Iliad* in which Achilles' shield, being forged on Olympus for the greatest combat of the greatest war, is intricately embossed with scenes from communal life "back home" and bound in by the River Ocean.[15]

I am not suggesting that these speeches and scenes work generically or mythically. This is certainly not the case in Shakespeare where all such speeches are the product of the speaker's sensibility and the age's obsession with metaphorical correspondences in the great chain of being. I would argue, however, that the impulse in a work to transcend the limits of finite time and space, in the right conditions, eventuates in myth and that we have the basics of such conditions in *Godot*; for on every level the play successfully contrives to be limitless, to escape the kind of clarity and specificity that Shakespeare takes pains to infuse into his containing speeches. It is not simply the speech itself, in other words, but the speech in its verbal surroundings. Imagine Lucky's monologue imported wholesale into a realistic comedy of manners, imagine him, say, as an escapee from a local asylum who finds his way into a Shavian drawing-room—and any conceivable mythic vibrations are drowned in down-to-earth hilarity. In the context of *Godot,* however, this pell-mell madness

15. On a somewhat humbler level, I am reminded of the business of the Jane Crofut letter which closes the first act of *Our Town*. You will recall that the address on the envelope began with the street number in Grovers Corners, passed up through New Hampshire, and ended in the Mind of God. It is a much more pleasant view of man's location in the cosmos but it does the same work of putting the One into the All.

functions very much like amnesia in the Beckett universe: it releases the character from bondage to a sensuous and temporal world. Does it not, in fact, create the same liberty of inference, or free association, that we have in Shakespeare when "mad" characters like Lear are set loose from society to conjure impossible nightmare worlds based crudely on the world of social fact? And could we not say that in such moments Shakespeare verges on the mythical?

Perhaps it comes down to this: thematic reductions like Williams's are valid readings which treat Lucky's monologue strictly as a species, however chaotic, of dialectical thinking (the command is "Think pig!" and the result is Thought); whereas I have been looking at the speech as a Kierkegaardian instance of mythic poetry, or at least mythic poetry coming to the aid of dialectic: that is, a narrative "reflection" of an Idea, addressed not to the understanding but to the imagination. Commanded to think, Lucky transcends his assignment; like the poet Plato, he "dreams into being" an image of "the spirit" of the world as seen in the infinite regression of its forms—much as the play at large, trading vaguely in theology, converts theology into mythic poetry.

III
The God in the Plot

So far I have been concerned mainly with ways in which the play manifests its mythic nature in isolated "parts" which I have sampled more or less randomly. I turn now to a set of problems relating to what might be summed up as *configuration,* or shapeliness: in a word, plot, conceived of as the arrangement of the events. There is no neat way to catch the play in its overall act, or to "pictorialize" it; but I can perhaps begin with an analogy from contemporary painting that will serve as a transition from what I have said about myth to what remains to be said about mythos.

Recently I happened to read David Sylvester's re-markable interviews with the Irish painter Francis Bacon, which offer just the sort of self-probe into a difficult art we would like to have from Beckett. In suggesting that there is a close affinity between Bacon and Beckett I do not imply that Beckett's people look like Bacon's or that Bacon would be a suitable illustrator of Beckett's plays (though he might be ideal for a "triptych" novel like *Comment c'est*). It is primarily the kind of art and the artist's relation to his art that concerns me. To begin, there are the obvious affinities of two contemporary artists with similar themes: a secular, or at least unreverent, preoccupation with religious subjects (notably the Crucifixion) and the anguish of creatural loneliness (the scream, silence). Moreover, the affective power of Bacon's painting rests on the Rorschach principle of making the most of resemblances ("This looks like its leg," "This may be its face," etc.). Bacon himself is given to throwing paint at the canvas and capitalizing on the result with selective elaboration. It is this accidental quality that creates the peculiar anxiety one feels before a Bacon painting: a yearning for clarity, a vague desire to improve the picture, though improvement of the picture would reduce the painting to banality; in other words, one wants to short-circuit the tension between the image Bacon gives you (Isabel Rawsthorne with an exploded jaw) and a possible real image that would be more faithful to "the subject."

More interesting, however, is Bacon's obsession with the difficulties and expressive qualities of the medium itself—the "despair" of making art at all, particularly when the artist is "outside a tradition" and must, so to speak, carve for himself.[1] Like Beckett, Bacon is deeply impatient with any critical attempt to reduce his art to ideas or intentions (even when an image is as inviting as a swastika on a uniform or a hypodermic needle in an arm). It is not a matter of there not being ideas and meanings in the art, but of the violence the act of interpretation does to what Bacon calls the "poignancy" or "vitality" of the art, its capacity to "unlock the valves of feeling" (p. 17). The question that explication invariably bypasses is the

1. David Sylvester, *Interviews with Francis Bacon* (London: Thames and Hudson, 1975), p. 43.

only one that is important to Bacon as an artist: "How can this thing be made so that you catch the mystery of appearance within the mystery of the making" (p. 105). The despair he speaks of, accordingly, is not the spiritual despair we associate with the Absurdists, but the constant danger of his losing the painting's mystery in the gravitational pull of illustration, on one hand, or abstraction, on the other. In short, the danger of becoming an interpreter of his own painting in the act of composing it. "Half my painting activity," he says, "is disrupting what I can do with ease" (p. 91). For the painter does not deal in meanings but in instincts; myths (like the Crucifixion) are "armatures" containing deep untranslatable affinities with human experience which become the hosts for the parasitical act of creation. Hence Bacon's paintings are concentrations on single figures rather than groups. "The moment there are several figures," he says, "the story begins to be elaborated. And the moment the story is elaborated, the boredom sets in; the story talks louder than the paint" (p. 22).

Unlike the painter, the dramatist cannot work handily with a single figure, Beckett's monologuists notwithstanding. But Bacon's "law" applies, in principle, to *Godot* about as well as it might apply to a one-man show like *Krapp's Last Tape*. Although there are four major characters in the play, they are used in such a way as to minimize any possibilities of story elaboration and to constitute what amounts to an "armature" or single portrait of "man in Essy." For one thing, Beckett's people condense, like Cain and Abel, into pairs, or cooperating identities, and this alone tends to subvert any conflict of competitive wills to a symbiotic tension: Vladimir and Estragon, as we say, form the complementary parts of individual man (mind/body, soul/appetite); Pozzo and Lucky form the complementary parts of the social hierarchy (master/servant, capitalist/philosopher), Pozzo's rope being less a tether or rein than a reciprocal bond and the visible symbol of civilization's unfortunate continuity.

Together, these two pairs bear somewhat the same relation as the two panels of a diptych: that is, if we were to draw "all mankind" into a polarity which would encompass extreme responses to life "under these conditions" (much as you would polarize responses to revenge at Elsinore into Hamlet and Laertes), we would arrive at these two pairs of "tied" characters who, in complementary tension, stand for the thrust of social history (man getting and spending, ruling and being ruled, rising and falling in the rhythm of change) and something, to recall Coleridge, we may describe as nostalgia for the Absolute (man outside, or wanting to be outside, the drama of mutability). Thus the logic of dramatic conflict gives way, at all points, to a logic of complementarity. Half the play's activity, you might say, is disrupting what it might do with ease: elaborate a plot with a problem, a complication, and a solution. All in all, the proper ancestor of this play might be *Prometheus Bound* in which we have a static situation offset by "arrivals" which deepen its significance through contrast (two versions of Zeus's wrath) rather than conflict. A nearer relative would be Chekhov's *Three Sisters,* reduced as follows: three sisters (variations of the same idea) live on a remote provincial estate, idling away the time in vague expectation of a more promising future; they are visited by a group of people who stir up emotions and bring on a crisis in which the dream is effectively flattened as a realistic option; the visitors leave and the sisters go on dreaming. What these plays have in common is the depiction of a beleaguered center of consciousness which is exposed, catalytically, to a series of encounters with an ongoing world which has its own problems of survival.

This is clearly a simplified reduction of the action: the truth is, you can not make an interesting play based strictly on the principle of complementarity, or contrast. Yet it is often pointed out that the French title, *En attendant Godot,* puts the emphasis squarely where it belongs (and where the English title does not): on the interim rather than on the expectation; not the act of waiting *for* something but the activity of waiting itself, in all its existential and spiritual dimensions. This is a reasonable assumption to the extent that the scenes of the play are descriptively aimed at exploring the conditions of waiting as opposed to the tension of expectation; moreover, if you disregard the play as a spiritual document and think of it as a behavioral description, it is a faithful account of the condition of boredom as most of us experience it. In fact, it is precisely its success in inducing a certain degree of boredom in its audience that makes the play interesting. I would not explain this seeming paradox by saying, as some have, that the play puts *us* in its own state of ontological estrangement, but rather along more basic lines: whether you are waiting for God or for a bus you are reduced to much the same state of suspension in an empty or unproductive interval, and this brings into play a special kind of attentiveness—on one hand, a scaling down of interim expectations and, on the other, a heightening of one's availability to interim reality. While waiting, one is like a motorist crossing a desert: any relief from the flat, undifferentiated coun- tryside (canyons, mesas, towns) is a waterhole for the thirsty eye.

This kind of attentiveness would scarcely last long in the theatre if nothing "interesting" were forthcom- ing. But one of the ingenious things about *Godot* is how skillfully it scales down our desire for dramatic "relief" and then consistently rewards us on the level to which we have become accustomed. This is effec- tively the discovery of Chekhov: in a still quiet room you can hear a whole adultery in a three-note melody and the deafening tick of the human soul in a glance at a watch. This is not a simple matter of "scaling down," as we know from dozens of plays liberally employing these low-keyed freedoms on situations with little or no soul to be listened to. But as far as pure plot mechanics go, *Godot* is a subtle exercise in the control of its audience's emotions. This is what I had in mind in something I wrote about the play several years ago:

Do we not encounter in a play as seemingly lacking in "drama" as *Waiting for Godot* a strong sense of the playwright as magician, putting himself in the worst possible predicament, "straitjacketing" himself with a plot in which "nothing happens," and then getting out of it, to the delight of an audience which knows that he *must,* otherwise it would not have been invited hither? And just as the magician's predicament conceals the very means of his escape, there is a respect in which Beckett has released *all* "plot" by appearing to have none at all; for he has found a form in which the most durable rhythms of tragedy, comedy, and farce are able to thrive side by side in an almost pure state. Thus, in *Godot,* "while waiting," we have such sure-fire theatre stuff (the very guts of Elizabethan drama) as quarrel and make-up scenes, song-and-dance scenes, scenes of cruelty, pathos, bawdry, rant and declamation, and one of the most original uses of the *deus ex machina* on record.[2]

Now that the flurry of admiration for the play's daring departure from tradition has passed (the argument ran that the play had no plot at all), I suspect that this was much too reactionary. I quote the passage, however, because it does shift our perspective from the metaphysics of waiting to the poetics of expecting.[3] And without further ado, I want to turn to the play's major intersection of plot and character, the event that is our biggest reward for having waited so patiently/impatiently for something to happen.

The arrival in the play of Pozzo and Lucky is indeed a sight for sore eyes. Here is a truly interesting shape

2. "The Case for Plot in Modern Drama," *Hudson Review* 20 (Spring 1967), pp. 58–59.
3. The quote also contains the seed of an idea to be expanded in the following chapter: the notion that "pure" forms of tragedy and comedy may be thriving "side by side" in the play.

(two strange men joined by a rope), to be inspected, fitted into the design. Here, for a time at least, we are thrown out of the routine of *en attendant*. The play is, after all, going the way of all plays, injecting a complicating ingredient (a Lovborg, a Vershinin) into its carefully established equation. Could we not say that it has suddenly lurched toward its promised future, that all the essentials advertised in the title are now accounted for and that the play will proceed to expand them narratively? That is, the play's most dramatic arrival turns out to be the right one.

The idea that Pozzo may be Godot has understandably never been a popular one, partly because Beckett himself (having entertained it in an early draft[4]) has flatly denied that Godot arrives. The question invites the most flagrant kind of over-reading, which is probably why Hugh Kenner and others find it a meaningless issue.[5] But I would like to pursue it here, cast temporarily in the role of a devilish advocate, because it seems a more complex question than we have assumed and one that bears as much on the play's art as on its ideas.

To begin with, to write it off one must ignore a good bit of flirting Beckett does with the possibility: the God phonetically concealed (along with the Italian cesspool) in Pozzo's name; his own statement, hardly trustworthy in itself, that he is "made in God's image" (in the French edition: *"De la même espèce que Pozzo!*

4. Colin Duckworth, *En attendant Godot,* (London: Harrap, 1966), pp. lx–lxi.
5. Hugh Kenner, *Samuel Beckett: A Critical Study,* (Berkeley and Los Angeles: University of California Press, 1973), p. 168.

D'origine divine!"[6]); the scene in which he hangs in misery between Vladimir and Estragon; the growing doubt that passes over Vladimir at the end when Estragon asks him if he is "sure" Pozzo isn't Godot, and Vladimir answers: "Not at all! *(Less sure.)* Not at all! *(Still less sure.)* Not at all!" Add to this, as a suggestion that at least an aura of sanctity surrounds Pozzo in this scene, Vladimir's line, "It seemed to me he saw us." That is, what but a kind of God-connectedness, or priestliness, is to be made of a blind man who sees?

This is the textual evidence, or most of it. But the best case can be made on very different grounds. It is not so much these obscure flirtations with divinity that give rise to the idea but the simple structural fact that Pozzo is what we get *instead* of Godot. Here the play is obliquely trading in the psychology of melodrama whereby we are led to expect, say, the detective arriving at the door and it turns out to be the killer. Or, in the play's own terms, we were expecting Godot, whom much of the exposition has been characterizing in terms of conventional Christian God-power, and what we get is a regional landowner, or burlesque of "local" God-power, who is not only utterly unsuitable as a "savior" but a simpering egotist as well. Even so, a god—of sorts: most evidently, the god whose rise is chronicled by Lewis Mumford in the slow historical displacement of God's eternal mystery by the technocracy whose symbol is the watch. For as the ensuing scene makes clear, Pozzo is a composite of medieval and modern, the incarnation of man *in transit,* with all

6. Duckworth, p. 17. The problematical nature of the line is discussed on p. cxiv.

due speed, via the shortest distance between two essential points: manor and marketplace. Thus, with Pozzo's entrance the long shadow of history falls over the stage, that is, the shadow of what has replaced God, the *deus in machina,* the new system, as we shall see later, in which man is both the measure and the measurer of all things.

But is there not another "elsewhere" behind this sociological symbolism? By a pattern-instruction (our natural "mania for symmetry," as Molloy says), Pozzo's visible role as the Godot of the secular world (symbolized by Lucky) holds the threat of spilling over into the spiritual world of the tramps as well: if Godot *there,* why not *here*? Again, I might recall the strategy by which Iago thoroughly creates a fixation of suspicion in Othello by simply uttering the words (on Cassio's departure from Desdemona) "I like not that." To Othello, these words obviously must come from his heart, or at least from his unvarnished instincts, and any denial to the contrary only drives the suspicion deeper. Thus, when Beckett has his tramps debate whether they are "tied to Godot" (repeating the verb six times) just prior to the entrance of Lucky on the end of Pozzo's rope, and then makes an elaborate fuss over whether Pozzo is Godot, he is introducing a possibility we cannot ignore thereafter. Whether the connection is real or not is not as important as that the play, in bothering to make it, is (as usual) having it both ways, throwing us what may be either a red herring or a curved ball, or both.

In other words, it is not necessary to have a real

Godot or even a bona fide Godot symbol in order to have (in a manner of speaking) a Godot arrival, a point about which the play can discourse on its most important subject. All that is needed is the structural equivalent of "a Coming." We do not know what Beckett had in mind; what is certain is that he was sophisticated in theological matters and to give his play its due we must assume that he was less interested in endorsing a God, or in denying his existence, than in "imitating" the enigma of the God-idea. In this sense, the arrival of Pozzo is a perfect blank check for anyone who wants to argue the question either way. If one abandons the Sunday School idea of a theistic God that has unconsciously afflicted the whole Godot question, all sorts of possiblities arise.[7] He might, for instance, be said to have arrived in principle: incorporeally, ambiguously, through "signs" or "works," as God characteristically

7. Many critical discussions understandably conflate God and Godot; but it is clear, as Colin Duckworth argues so well, that God and Godot are "quite separate entities" (p. cxiii). For example, Estragon does not say, "Do you think Godot sees me?" Obviously, the play invites *us* to blend the two "entities" and to think of Godot as a symbol of God. But it is precisely from the distinction the play draws between God and Godot that it derives its most serious theological dimension. One can legitimately bring to the play all sorts of concepts of God, or the Divine, which have nothing to do with waiting for a savior to arrive *in time*. To affirm categorically that God does not arrive, and probably does not even exist, because Godot does not arrive is to make exactly the sort of mistake Vladimir and Estragon make in depending on Godot for their salvation, rather than asserting their own "prerogatives" or adopting a less self-oriented understanding of God. This is perhaps a severe way of looking at the problem. My point is not to argue

does in the Scriptures after the Fall; he might be a divinity, as Martin Buber would say, who addresses us only through events. I suspect that if someone like Augustine, who has a rather high threshold for paradox, were faced with the problem of justifying Pozzo with Christian doctrine he would have no more trouble seeing a *figura* of Christ in him than he did with Adam, particularly in the scene in which Pozzo literally stumbles and falls in the shade of the tree and then is raised, arms outstretched, between the two "thieves." In other words, you can get out of the Pozzo arrival whatever theology you bring to it. To be truly outrageous, imagine what a "Lutheran" interpreter might make of it in the light of Luther's extraordinary humanization of Christ in "The Epistle to the Galatians": here Christ is seen as coming "wrapped in the sins of the whole world, . . . bearing all our iniquities, . . . the greatest transgressor, murderer, adulterer, thief, rebel, blasphemer, &c. that ever was or could be in all the world."[8]

---

this, or any position but to show how positions have a way of answering only some of the questions the play raises as a thorough equation of God-man relations. Part of Beckett's genius as a playwright/thinker (whatever his private beliefs) is that he keeps God and Godot in two separate "compartments" of thought while seeming to equate them (as in an allegory); and from this fact you can spin any number of contradictory theories—as many, perhaps, as there are believers or atheists to invent them. It would be hard to name any other play of the century which opens, and leaves ajar, as many doors to the Divine as this one does.

8. Martin Luther, *A Commentary on St. Paul's Epistle to The Galatians* (London: James Clarke, 1953), p. 269ff. I am not suggesting

These would be gratuitous connections if there were not strong evidence that the whole Pozzo/Lucky plot is there primarily to provoke a confrontation between Vladimir and Estragon and some form of ultimate value. Pozzo's character as a rather silly man is not very important beside the catalytic value of his injection into the sphere of waiting. And in this sense he is the instrument of a higher power, call it Godot, God, or the playwright's power as creator of a contained universe. In fact, there is a respect in which Pozzo's very weakness as a man enhances his function as an instrument of this power: what happens to him, the change he undergoes between his two passings, as we shall see

---

that there is anything further in this idea; nor am I trying to get in an ingenious reading on the ground that I plan to throw it out. But Luther's interpretation of Christ as the total sinner, crucified with sinners, illustrates the extreme sense in which the natural ambiguity of religious symbolism can be converted to almost any end. Once you blur the distinction between a God who takes on man's sins and sin itself, it is only a matter of how far you wish to venture into paradox. For example, I might have cited Borges' idea (perhaps inspired by the Gnostic *Gospel of Judas*) that God did not come to earth as Christ at all: He became "a man completely, a man to the point of infamy, a man to the point of being reprehensible—all the way to the abyss. . . . He chose an infamous destiny: He was Judas." "Three Versions of Judas," (*Ficciones* [New York: Grove Press, 1962], p. 108). My point is that the attraction the play has for so many different kinds of readers lies in the convertibility of its images: they are, as I've said, cooperatively docile. I suspect that Beckett's oft-repeated remark that he "takes no sides" in what the play means springs from a fear, like Bacon's, that in exercising the persuasive authority of authorship, he will bias the paradoxical suspension of ideas he had built into the design of his play.

in the next chapter, produces the effect of a Judgment for Vladimir and Estragon, an encounter with what Tillich calls "ultimate concern." If Pozzo and Lucky stand for the community of men in Act I, in Act II they stand for the plight of individual man, the condition to which man is inevitably subject: the action of time.

It would be an absurd distortion of the play to see any of these interpretations as being on Beckett's mind, consciously or otherwise. The idea is not that Pozzo is any of these things, but that where gods are concerned, and the theologians (or playwrights) who contemplate them, paradox is never far away; and there is nothing in the books (or in this play) to suggest that they keep their appointments according to human expectations. Christ, we might recall, came in the least expected form and one of the consequences of his doing so was that the whole burden of perceiving his divinity was thrown onto man's Faith, or what we might appropriately call his second sight. In fact, on a simple moralistic level something like this is going on in the second act of the play: it could be argued that Vladimir and Estragon finally flunk, or all but flunk, a test by putting their appointment with Godot, and its hoped-for rewards, above any humanistic, or "Christian," concern for Pozzo's cries for help ringing in their ears. (Here our theological text might be either Buber or Camus). Pozzo and Lucky stand, at this point, for suffering humanity. Hence the validity of the Crucifixion symbolism in this scene; for in standard theology the Crucifixion is endlessly repeated each time man sins, and it is not necessary to be a

Christian (witness Camus) to see the validity of this symbolism in a purely secular context. From this standpoint, the whole character of the vigil is opportunistic, to say the least: Vladimir and Estragon behave, for the most part, like the thief in the Lukian Crucifixion who said, in effect, "If you're Christ, get us out of this!"

In any event, insofar as the play is dealing seriously with the God theme, whether it is being "religious" about it or not, we should credit it with doing thorough justice to God-power and it is self-evident that any open personification of God, or Godot, or conversely any open denial of his existence, would be both simplistic and historically premature. What the play gives us instead, in perfect self-consistency, is exactly the kind of Janus-sign that is implicit in its master paradox of the two thieves. Or, to carry self-consistency a step further, we could say that Pozzo is to the action of the play what the single tree is to its scene. To illustrate: in one of his sermons, Augustine has a wonderful parable which recovers the orthodox figural idea of Christ as the Tree of Life: imagine two trees, he says, one vigorous and one withered. In the winter, the vigorous tree looks exactly like the withered tree:

For in winter time, both the tree which is vigorous and [the tree] which is withered, are both bare of the beauty of the leaves, both are empty of the adornment of fruit. Summer will come, and there will be a distinction between the trees. The living root puts forth leaves and is pregnant with fruit;

the withered one will remain as barren in the heat of summer as it was in the winter. . . . So our summer is the coming of Christ; our winter the occultation of Christ; our summer the revelation of Christ.[9]

What we have in *Godot,* of course, is not a "revelation" but a compromise: begrudgingly, the withered tree of Act I puts forth "four or five leaves" in Act II, scarcely a pregnancy, but then not a barrenness—a reasonable percentage at today's odds.[10] In any case, it is not a question of whether the tree announces a coming or a departure, or whether Pozzo is a symbol of Christ or Anti-Christ, of God or of Mammon, or even a conflation of the two (God as Overlord), but of the play mimetically obeying its own premise that "Nothing is certain." God is not absent from the play; he is simply not quite present. He is, as Augustine is never at a loss to point out, a hidden God, not a missing one, and he peeps out of Pozzo, and the tree, with just enough insistence to keep himself immanent in a play that can neither admit him nor do without him.

9. From Sermon XXXVI, iv, 4. Quoted in *An Augustine Synthesis,* arranged by Erich Przywara (New York: Harper, 1958), pp. 291–292.

10. In manuscript and in the French editions of the play the tree is *"couvert de feuilles"* in Act II. According to Colin Duckworth, Beckett and Roger Blin (in the premiere production) settled on a "few sparse leaves" because it was theatrically "more effective" and this reduction of hope was carried over into subsequent English editions (*En attendant Godot,* pp. liii–liv). I am obviously not implying that Beckett was following (or even aware of) Augustine's "distinction" between the vigorous and the withered trees.

IV
The Fool of Time

The "summer" in which *Godot* takes place does produce a "revelation" of a kind, but in order to coax it out of hiding we must approach the play on a purely secular path. These same echoes of divinity in Pozzo contain still another "Passion" that has nothing to do with his being a god, in any form, but with the fact that he passes drastically through a god's hands: he has the mark of Cain upon him. Put simply, in Pozzo we have the stark outline of tragedy itself. I must preface this idea by returning to my earlier suggestion (Chapter 3) that in *Godot* "the most durable rhythms of tragedy, comedy, and farce are able to thrive side by side in an almost pure state." If we were trying to justify the play as a tragicomedy the most obvious evidence would be found in the overall tonality of its words and acts which I have described as an oxymoronic fusion of the serious and the light. What I propose, further, is that on the structural level the play offers a collision of the essentially pure energies of comedy and tragedy. For convenience, let us break the play down into two plots—not in the strict Elizabethan sense of there being two concurrent story lines, as in *Lear,* but in the sense that we have two sets of characters with independent destinies which happen to cross in the stream of generic time and space. On one hand, we have a plot that is derived from the vaudeville principle of the comic routine whose only logic of arrangement seems to be that the routines should ideally occur in the most entertaining order. This, of course, is the Vladimir/ Estragon plot which might potentially go in circles forever. On the other hand, we have the Pozzo/Lucky plot in which we detect a strict irreversible order of events based on the tragic idea of the "lamentable fall." That is, in the two given events of Pozzo's career (to ignore Lucky for the moment) we can trace the rising and falling slopes of the classical *De casibus* pyramid which dates back to Cain's father and is passed up through hundreds of "sad stories" of the deaths of kings and magistrates who, in one way or another, set themselves up for a mortal blow and, sure enough, receive it. The structure is almost invariably the same and it is modeled, as I say, on the geometry of the pyramid: there is the *hubris* slope in which arrogance and pride are set forth as the "sins" which make the protagonist ripe for the fall; and the *reversal* slope in which we see him brought low by Fortune. Obviously we must do a lot of discounting for Pozzo's clear lack of heroic stature and sensibility, but then we are in a universe where these would be alien qualities, to say the least. But if we squint out the refinements we associate with "great" tragedy, this outline emerges as a parodistic after-image of all lamentable falls from Adam forward. Considered as subplot, one might say that Pozzo is the play's "tragic relief"; he comes stumbling onto this vaudeville stage straight out of the corridors of dramatic history, literally (in Edmund's words) the catastrophe from an old play.

Viewed from this literary distance, Pozzo's fortunes
take on another mythic significance which opens us to
the play's subtlest level of oscillation. What, we must
ask, are we to make of the fact that someone in this
otherwise "eventless" play undergoes the kind of radical change that the action of tragedy was, in another
age, designed to imitate? What does Pozzo's blindness
mean?[1] What is the nature of the world-order it exem-
plifies? These are complex questions which must wait
upon an examination of the main plot for thorough
answers. But we may begin along these lines: if we
isolate Pozzo and Lucky from the rest of the play
—thinking it, for the moment, out of existence—we
see immediately that as citizens of an old-fashioned

1. There is, of course, the problem of whether Pozzo is really
blind. Colin Duckworth examines the pros and cons of this idea
and more or less leaves it an open question (*En attendant Godot*
[London: Harrap, 1966] (p. lxii and pp. ciii–civ). While there is a
possibility that Pozzo is faking the blindness—in which case the
line "It seemed to me he saw us" would have to be interpreted as
outright suspicion on Vladimir's part—I think such a reading seriously diminishes the play. For one thing, it requires that we make
all sorts of subtextual inferences about Pozzo's motives; for
another, it seriously cheapens the emotional import of the
"When!" speech in Act II, and Vladimir's soliloquy ("Was I sleeping while the others suffered?") becomes the outgrowth of a lie (if
not a practical joke) —moreover a lie that the play makes no dramatic use of. Even if Beckett had this dimly in mind at some early
point (it was clearly not there when he advised Paul Curran to play
Pozzo as being blind in the Royal Court production of 1964: see
Duckworth, p. civ), are we not obliged to interpret the ambiguities
in Pozzo's character in a light that will do the play the fullest
service? For example, would one want to interpret Hamlet as a
homosexual simply because he makes a considerable protestation
of love to Horatio? The textual evidence for fakery on Pozzo's part
seems about this substantial.

world they are also the subjects of old-fashioned gods. Unlike the Godot of the title, for whom one waits (and waits), the divine force of Pozzo's world does not operate from the heights of apathy, athambia, and aphasia. He may finally, like Godot, be inscrutable, but if gods are known by their acts (are located *in* acts) — and this is normally their only visibility in tragedy — we must conclude that he is a strict and efficient purveyor of the human scene, which is, as always in tragedy, a scene of misery. The conduct of this misery is delegated (by Pozzo's own citation) to the goddess Fortune, who is of course the personification of Mutability. Above all, her work is precise and thorough. She operates on the slender moral principle that any violation of proportion or degree is sufficient to set the full circle of her wheel in motion.

The obvious question, at this point, is, What is the violation? In what sense could we say that Pozzo has *caused* his own ruin? In Act II, he tells Vladimir that he "woke up one fine day blind as Fortune," which suggests that if he has done anything to deserve his fate the point is lost on him. Moreover, there is the fact that Lucky has been struck dumb, presumably in the same blow, and it is surely safe to say that thinking out loud occasionally is scarcely an offense that should rouse a slumbering god. I would claim, however, that this is a narrow perspective on the disaster and that there is a kind of rightness or perfection in this double fall that has less to do with moral justice than with tragic logic. Here it would be helpful to return to our contrast of the real and the mythical. We have said that the elaboration of causal features is the province of plays and fictions immersed deeply in "an organic process of nature," in the content of a history (Shakespeare, Ibsen, *et al.*). Macbeth dies because he listened to certain voices on a bloody afternoon. From such causes, tragic events work their way out. The triumph of a play like *Macbeth,* it should be said, does not rest in its successful pursuit of a moral imperative but in the superaddition of an independent factor that is summed up in Johnson's phrase "the just representation of general nature," which is to say, the objective chronicling of a "particular" psychology (to use Hamlet's word), which happens, in particular circumstances, to express a general law of behavior.

If what I have said about *Godot's* mythic style is true, we should expect to find little more than a negligent theft of the tragic, along the lines of the play's theft of the Crucifixion. Myth, to recall Barthes, is speech stolen and restored, and what is restored is "no longer that which was stolen." For example, the old cartoon of the cannibal who, having dined on the missionary, now wears his spectacles as an ornament—the spectacles, in this new context, being the "comic" remnant of a serious misapprehension of reality. All told, what we have in the Pozzo/Lucky plot is such a cartoon: tragedy's radical sequence reduced to a remnant, to a before-after advertisement for the world's power to get even (and then some), and inserted into the continuum of a vaudeville routine. ("He's all humanity," Estragon quips, falling unknowingly upon an old truth.) What is missing, what was not stolen, is the development (Acts II, III, and IV) in which the terrible disproportion between cause and effect, beginning and end, is made "logical" by the contingent march of events. The true remnant of the tragic, of course, is the blindness itself, that quintessential emblem of tragic man, which may be described punningly as a loss of sight brought on by a lack of vision. More than that, blindness is the very knot of the tragic paradox, binding cause and effect into a unity. For when it comes, hindsight is never far behind:

When! When! One day, is that not enough for you, one day he went dumb, one day I went blind, one day we'll go deaf, one day we were born, one day we shall die, the same day, the same second, is that not enough for you? *(Calmer.)* They give birth astride of a grave, the light gleams an instant, then it's night once more. *(He jerks the rope.)* On!
Exeunt Pozzo and Lucky. . . .

There is more to be said about this speech's crucial function in the *other* plot, but here it suffices to note that it is a classic recognition, as obligatory in *De casibus* tragedy as the reversal itself. It is a very different cut from anything in Act I; there is no other speech in the play (apart from Vladimir's echo of it) as uncompromisingly serious as this last "grave" note on which Pozzo leaves the play. What is perhaps so stunning about the speech is that one has the sense of a violent rent in the play's tragicomic veil through which we suddenly see what has been behind it all along. Admittedly, it is a dark recognition: it suggests that blindness, the loss of all sensory security, and of life itself, are the whims of Fortune, who has a sense of humor suspiciously like that of the Absurd. But the fact is, it is essentially the same tragic knowledge that we find regularly in time-collapsing speeches from Richard II's "numb'ring clock" ("I wasted time, and now doth time waste me") to Macbeth's "brief candle." In its moral bleakness, it is much more akin to Macbeth's findings insofar as the emphasis falls not upon the culpability of the time-waster but on the universal fact that man himself is the fool of time. In any case, it is rarely a matter of moral enlightenment in these speeches, which are always bland when reduced to an idea, but of an attitude of gained respect for what Pozzo calls "the things of time," which are hidden from the blind "too"—meaning, one assumes, that blindness does not illuminate: it simply puts the seal on a destiny that began in a "blind" thrusting forth of the self. What emerges from the speech, finally, is not wisdom but a Stoic relinquishment of the self to the uses of the world, such as they are.

This is something that the more stable characters of tragedy are not privileged to realize, except vicariously through the pale rhetoric of the scapegoat hero. One earns this attitude only by becoming the fool of Fortune, which is to say, by mounting a wheel that is also, for all intents, the dial of a clock. Thus, applying tragedy's tit-for-tat logic, one might expect to find the cause of Pozzo's blindness in some prior act of misapprehension, or myopia, such as those committed on a grander scale by Oedipus or Gloucester, the foremost of the tribe who cannot "see" until it is too late. It is doubtful that anyone could have identified Pozzo in Act I as a tragedy-in-the-making. But if we read his career backwards, after the fact, it is not hard to see wherein he deserves what he gets. For one thing, his conduct reeks of petty pride: he behaves like a king (or a braggart soldier imitating a Tamburlaine), and it is axiomatic in drama that anyone who preens is bound to come unfeathered. But this is not sufficiently sharp, and Beckett has further focused his flaw in a single speech in which he "ripens" before our eyes into a true fool of Time and Fortune:

What is there so extraordinary about it? Qua sky. It is pale and luminous like any sky at this hour of the day. *(Pause.)* In these latitudes. *(Pause.)* When the weather is fine. *(Lyrical.)* An hour ago *(he looks at his watch, prosaic)* roughly *(lyrical)* after having poured forth even since *(he hesitates, prosaic)* say ten o'clock in the morning *(lyrical)* tirelessly torrents of red and white light it begins to lose its effulgence, to grow pale *(gesture of the two hands lapsing by stages)* pale, ever a little paler, a little paler until *(dramatic pause, ample gesture of the two hands flung wide apart)* pppfff! finished! it comes to rest. But—*(hand raised in admonition)*—but behind this veil of gentleness and peace night is charging *(vibrantly)* and will burst upon us *(snaps his fingers)* pop! like that! *(his inspiration leaves him)* just when we least expect it. *(Silence. Gloomily.)* That's how it is on this bitch of an earth.

This speech is one of the best examples of how the play manages to sound its big themes while seeming to be mired down in idle diversion. Of all the things Beckett could have given Pozzo to discourse on he chose the transit of the sun, the God of all gods, the Eye of all eyes, the light that burned darkness from the face of the deep. In short, the hubris lies in the disparity between speaker and subject: in this world of meager aspiration, Pozzo commits the rhetorical equivalent of Icarus's overestimation of the power of a homemade machine—he would clock the firmament with a genuine half-hunter. In fact, if we put the speech side by side with the great "firmament" speech Lucky will unleash later in the scene, we see the inevitable difference between pupil and master. The vision of "the great cold the great dark" which Lucky conjures with considerable terror is reduced by Pozzo to an elocutionary performance. Two versions of the same process—the conversion of heat and light to cold and darkness—which for good measure is projected scenically on the backdrop at the end of each act: "The light suddenly fails. In a moment it is night. The moon rises at back, mounts in the sky, stands still, shedding a pale light on the scene."

Pitiful as the speech is, there is something very Renaissance about its correspondence of the human, the natural and the supranatural worlds. The simple merging of day into night is here given apocalyptic proportions: Night, in short, becomes a form of Nemesis, cloaked in a "gentle" natural process. The sky-show may begin at ten o'clock in the morning but it will end "outside time" with a cosmic whimper. It should be said that Pozzo gets a part of his own symbolism, insofar as the charge of night "when we least expect it" is equated with life "on this bitch of an earth." But it remains a bad recitation of a prophesy, a "fantastic trick" against high heaven which heaven will play back in turn, beginning with the theft of Pozzo's watch at the end of the scene.

Sum it up like this: if you were Fortune (temporarily

on loan to tragicomedy) and were casting about among men for an excuse to exercise your specialty (radical irony), what better opportunity than this man who not only speaks of matters far above his head but ignorantly pronounces his own sentence while doing so. Here is an almost ideal victim, a prophet without foresight: not a "native Theban," it is true; but then this is tragicomedy where things are tempered for the mixed effect.

Finally, there remains the question of Lucky: How can we account for his disaster, if not as the wanton malice of the Absurd? Surely he is innocent of the sin of Pride and we may exonerate him on moral grounds. But this has never removed anyone in tragedy from the path of Fortune's "massy wheel." "The cess of majesty"—assuming we can see at least a caricature of majesty in Pozzo—"Dies not alone, but like a gulf doth draw/What's near it with it." We have said that above all else Fortune is precise and thorough. Thus she embodies the world's full capacity for destruction by dramatizing the simple and real fact that nothing in a disturbed universe is exempt; the sun, to use an appropriate figure of Max Scheler's, shines (or frowns) on the good and the bad alike, and this is what makes tragedy possible.[2] To ask, therefore, why Lucky is struck dumb is to ask why Cordelia is hanged or Ophelia driven to suicide. Lucky is the social context of Pozzo's fall, the ground of repercussion without which tragedy would remain a simple lesson in "Thou shalt not" morality. He is, if you will, the dying of

2. Max Scheler, "On the Tragic," *Cross-Currents* 4, no. 2 (Winter 1954): 184.

Thebes, the howling widows of Scotland, the England that groans. In short, he represents not only innocence victimized by Pride but the responsive counterblow of Fate which plunges the world into misery without respect to innocence or guilt.

In drawing this analogy with tragedy, I have tried to show only what the play awakens of our "racial" memory of a prior fictional form. There are probably other possibilities. In other words, if we were to walk back along the mythic road on which *Godot* takes place, we would encounter numerous shapes from scriptural, historical, and literary memory which might be called ancestors of the scene enacted before us in the play. Some of these shapes would be vague and partial, some more distinct, and we would pass many intersections at which still other mythic ancestors would cross our path momentarily, as Pozzo and Lucky cross it twice and, in the world of imaginary reality, may be said to have lived other stages of their lives between crossings. Only in a general sense would this be a chronological journey back through time, for there is a vein of the ancestral which exists by virtue of class resemblance.

If anything, I have simplified the meanings and memory-traces inherent in the Pozzo/Lucky situation. There is, finally, no accounting for the depth of a literary symbol or a single figure sprung from myth; this is less a compliment to the play than to literature itself, any part of which, in Northrop Frye's fine phrase, leads us to the still center of words. What I have suggested, in illustration of the point, is that there are two primary ways of looking at Pozzo's fate: two mythic analogues, one scriptural and one secular, both grounded in the same shape, both leading to the same destiny. By a slight ocular shift, the Agony of the Cross becomes the Agony of the Scapegoat, which are but two primal variations of the archetype of sinful and suffering man.

V
The Imposed Situation

Taken as a whole, the play acts out no such thesis as I have advanced. But if we had only Pozzo and Lucky this is what we would have: a deterministic plot with a beginning, an implicit middle, and an end—the stuff of tragic biography.

A further corollary to this idea is suggested by some pertinent remarks on fictional plots made by Frank Kermode in *The Sense of An Ending*. A plot, he says, is "an organization that humanizes time by giving it form," and its simplest model can be found in the *tick-tock* of a clock: *tick* is a beginning, "a humble genesis," and *tock* an ending, "a feeble apocalypse"; *tick* produces a "lively expectation" of *tock, tock* "bestow[s] upon the whole duration and meaning." Behind this analogy is the familiar concept of time known as *kairos*, "a point in time filled with significance, charged with a meaning derived from its relation to the end"; *kairoi* are "historical moments of intemporal significance," or events that transcend temporality by "bundling together perception of the present, memory of the past, and expectation of the future, in a common organization." Over against *kairos* is a second and opposed concept of time, which is *chronos:* "passing time," or "waiting time," "humanly uninteresting successiveness," the empty intervals between and around *tick* and *tock*.[1]

In principle at least, my idea is probably already self-evident: the two plots of *Godot* (Pozzo/Lucky and Vladimir/Estragon) bear the same dialectical relationship to each other as *kairos* and *chronos*. That is, they dramatize antithetical concepts of being-in-time. The drama of Pozzo and Lucky is a *tick-tock* (a half-hunter with deadbeat escapement) inserted into the undifferentiated flux of Vladimir's and Estragon's vigil. This is what, among other things, gives the vigil its interest, relieves it of tedium, tells its time, much as a falling meteor "tells" the emptiness of space. The accompanying diagram shows how we might visualize the scheme. The solid lines represent actual stage time, the dotted lines the trajectory of the characters' careers outside the play. The pyramid, as we have said, is the Pozzo/Lucky plot, marked at the apex by a peripety, or moment of reversal in which Pozzo is

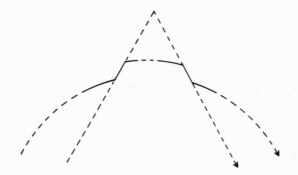

1. Frank Kermode, *The Sense of An Ending: Studies in The Theory of Fiction* (New York: Oxford University Press, 1967), pp. 45–47.

struck blind and Lucky dumb; the arc is the Vladimir/
Estragon plot, a self-repeating circle, briefly displaced
into linearity (on either slope) by the collision. In short,
two opposed yet complementary geometries of
experience—chronology versus chronicity—are
brought into conjunction to form a single plot which,
in effect, is a metaphorical tension of two deep structures, each carrying its own archetypal charge.

Behind one, as I have said, is the central mythos of
tragedy, or that reading of experience which imitates,
in personal and secular terms, the coming about of
Apocalypse. There is more to be said about how this
Apocalypse bears on the overall idea of the play; but
before we approach that problem something must be
said about the geometry and mimetic nature of the
Vladimir/Estragon plot.

Not only are there two plots in the play but, more
importantly, there are two kinds of plots. By way of
revealing their inherent differences, I shall put them
into a somewhat procrustean antithesis that will take
us, temporarily, out of the play proper. As a conven-
ient model for this purpose, I have chosen an antithesis proposed by David L. Miller in an essay titled
"Orestes: Myth and Dream as Catharsis." Briefly, the
relevant part of Miller's argument runs like this: there
are, on the extremes, two kinds of cathartic drama.
The first type is the ritual mimetic, or Aristotelian,
which imitates a terrifying action "in such a way as to
distinguish past causes of the present situation."[2] Plays

2. In *Myths, Dreams, and Religion,* ed. Joseph Campbell (New
York: Dutton, 1970), p. 36.

like *Oedipus* and *King Lear* capture "a critical dramatic moment in the playing out of a ritual pattern" and, in doing so, purge the audience through an act of clarification and explanation. The characteristic flaw of the hero is hubris which, in its Greek etymology, means "to run riot," "to prance and bray"; hubris is "the mania of an ego's vertigo, endlessly spinning about its own center" (p. 38).

The second type (and it is important to bear in mind that Miller is developing a polarity, not a set of exclusive categories) is the lyrical *poietic* drama which is based not upon a critical moment but on "a total metaphor of meaning"; it is "a dream" that "complements the spectator's waking life" and catharsis (in plays like *The Bacchae* and *The Tempest*) takes the form of "unification and completion." The characteristic flaw of the hero is not hubris but *erinus,* or "tempestuousness," literally possession by the Furies (pp. 38–39). Both hubris and erinus (extensions, according to Miller, of the Apollonian-masculine and the Dionysian-feminine principles) are the energizing forces by which drama works its way to catharsis.

The Orestes myth comes into the picture in the merger of these two strains, and here I diverge from Miller's thesis for my own purposes. For Orestes, considered at some remove from specific texts, seems to me rather the perfect paradigm of the hero whose ego is eclipsed by his destiny: as a man doomed by one god (Apollo) to murder his mother and to suffer the punishment of madness by another (Demeter), he is doubly possessed, trapped in a cosmic scheme in which his character and will are all but an after thought. He is virtually vacant of psychological depth.[3] As it comes down to us, the distinguishing feature of Orestes' story is that of a life channeled to the exclusion of all else but the commission of an unnatural act. He is groomed for mother-murder. I would put Orestes against a hubris-driven hero like Oedipus, the world's greatest example of predestined unnaturalism, insofar as Oedipus's story is primarily one of recognition and discovery. With Orestes, recognition loses its centrality in the drama and is relegated to a straightening out of identities. The emphasis is rather on the carrying out of the dreadful command and the subsequent punishment: man is *the instrument* of the gods. And it is in keeping with this emphasis that the *Oresteia* should end in a trial in which Orestes is virtually a bystander in a far more urgent case of divine gerrymandering.

I grant the danger in such oppositions. There is so much here we could question (for example, Exactly what *is* catharsis? When is emotional response to drama *not* cathartic?). Obviously, we have left out of account the whole middle range of drama brought on by other forms of error or flaw—mistaken identities,

3. In this sense, Electra differs from her brother in the overlay of mother-hatred which one finds in her character between Sophocles and Freud. In fact, the ambiguity of Electra's character suggests an even clearer sense in which the erinutic and the hubristic flaws can be collapsed into each other—how, in other words, the ego might give itself divine pretensions, as in those stories of conquerors or murderers who dignify their ambitions by claiming they have been ordained from on high ("It is God's will that I take this throne"). But insofar as these remain deceitful or casuistical maneuvers, they are hubristic in origin. In short, there is a basic difference between getting God on your side, as Electra seems to do, and having him there, whether you want him or not, as Orestes does.

codes of love and honor, social victimization, and so on. And it is more often than not the case in even the purest tragedy that elements of both hubris and erinus are hopelessly confused. But I am not concerned here with these terms as Greek inventions but as alternative psychologies of playmaking which persist as cowpaths through the whole of dramatic history. Considered as hypothetical purities which bear in a revealing way on the *double* genesis of our play, on its deepest constructional logic, I would summarize them as follows: the hubris situation poses the dilemma of what happens when an individual takes things into his own hands and disregards the laws intended to safeguard collective rights. The emphasis falls on the self-corruptibility of the hero, the internal drives that "disturb the universe" and awaken the gods (or society) to retribution. There is, in short, an implicit guilt which can be laid at no other doorstep. Hubris drama is the drama of *actual* sin in the sense of sin originating with the sinner, and it is therefore the ideal mirror not only for magistrates but for restless citizens as well. The dilemma posed by the erinutic drama, on the other hand, is that of inherited or "original" sin, the sin for which one is not directly responsible but inevitably accountable. The reason both are inevitably present in tragedy (not to mention in most drama, including comedy) is that neither one nor the other can fully account for the human predicament, and the dominance of either one tends to produce a polemical bias which destroys the equilibrium we associate with tragic art. Hubris alone throws the scale toward "moral lesson" with the implication that all would be right with the world were it not for the fact that bad men live in it; erinus alone throws the scale toward a fatalistic view of the world: the cause of disaster is in the "scheme of things," which is to say in the sinful and all-powerful gods who kill us for their sport.

I have gone into some detail on this matter, at the risk of losing sight of the play, because it seems to me that the equilibrium of *Godot*—the source of its remarkable durability as a portrait of man in historical/ spiritual time—rests upon a fusion of these two energies. This does not account for its quality as a play, but it does account for its seriousness, its comprehensiveness. And it also helps to explain how it reaches back in time and carries—as all plays do, in one way or another—its own racial memory of earlier forms which persist necessarily because they are our best language for talking on the subject of man.

The point is, of course, that Vladimir and Estragon belong to the erinutic tradition. Or, to put it less formidably, theirs is a drama of what Jan Kott calls the "imposed situation."[4] Kott is referring specifically to *Hamlet,* but the term applies equally well to countless god-infected heroes from Orestes forward who are trapped in a cosmic plan in which the needs of the self count for nothing, or next to nothing, against the keeping of a divinely made "appointment." Obviously there is a world of difference between killing kinsmen and killing time. What concerns me here is not the business end of the appointment but its structure of causality: the submission of human will to outside

4. Jan Kott, *Shakespeare Our Contemporary,* trans. Boleslaw Taborski (Garden City, N.Y.: Doubleday, 1964), p. 60.

forces, or what we might describe as being hoist by someone else's petard. It is easy to see why the imposed situation has been so congenial to the drama at large. As we know from the Orestes plays alone, it was a perfect crucible for the reevaluation of prerogatives both human and divine. As a plot situation, it undergoes a gradual secularization from Greek gods and heroes to Renaissance rulers and their subjects, to the oppressive modern society and its "little" victims. Midway in the evolution we find Hamlet who is the most complete classical prototype of the so-called Absurd hero because he so encyclopedically asks a whole set of questions we can sum up under the heading of self-determination. *Hamlet* passes into more recent literature through many doors, becoming, as it were, a fractured myth, any part of which seems capable of generating its own modern progeny. The most notable is probably Dostoevsky's Underground Man whose "Notes" have been called (by Walter Kaufmann[5]) the best overture to Existentialism ever written. It is effectively at this point that revenge (as a God- or Father-ordained act) becomes culturally outmoded and rebellion moves to the fore as the drive behind the plot—that is, rebellion as a self-defense against *any* duty imposed by moral or societal pressure. Beyond this we reach the sluggish delta of nineteenth-century realism which Northrop Frye has characterized as the study of "the frustrating and smothering of human activity by the combined pressure of a reactionary society without and a disor-

5. Walter Kaufmann, *Existentialism from Dostoevsky to Sartre* (New York: Meridian Books, 1958), p. 14.

ganized soul within."[6] Long before this time, of course, we have lost any trace of an archetype, properly speaking, but it is through the filter of this fallen world that any return to an archetype bearing on god-man relations would have to pass.

To sum it up: the distinction I would draw between our two plots—and of course there are other ways of putting them into relief—is quite close to Georg Lukacs's antithesis of tragic and modern drama on the principle of "constructing the guilt" or "building bridges between the deed and the doer."[7] On one hand, the world represented by Pozzo and Lucky implies a concept of cause and effect, of sin and punishment, or at least of Fortune striking with some justification. The world of Vladimir and Estragon, on the other, is one in which Pride does not go before a Fall but before a vast silence. Hence the impression of an unchanging essential: of time without content, chronicity without chronology. Everything happens, as it were, at a distance and leaks through the surface of a diversionary routine which is the last refuge of the dying ego. There is only a vestige of the oppressive society in the form of thugs who administer unprovoked beatings under cover of night, and all that remains of the demanding god is a dim historical memory with barely enough gravitational pull to keep his "subjects" in a vague orbit of supplication. But the Vladimir/Estragon plot is intelligible largely as a "last

6. *Anatomy of Criticism: Four Essays* (Princeton, N.J.: Princeton University Press, 1957), p. 285.
7. George Lukacs, "The Sociology of Modern Drama," trans. Lee Baxandall, in *Tulane Drama Review* 9, No. 4 (Summer 1965): 150.

bridge" in this whole burdensome history of obligation and ego-frustration. It is in this sense that Lukacs's "Sociology of Modern Drama," written in 1909, seems almost as valid as a prophecy of Samuel Beckett as it is an "Aristotelian" commentary on the drama that had already been written. For instance, as a last bridge between deed and doer, consider *Godot* in the light of this passage:

This is the [modern] dramatic conflict: man as merely the intersection point of great forces, and his deeds not even his own. Instead something independent of him mixes in, a hostile system which he senses as forever indifferent to him, thus shattering his will. And the why of his acts is likewise never wholly his own, and what he senses as his inner motivating energy also partakes of an aspect of the great complex which directs him toward his fall. The dialectical force comes to reside more exclusively in the idea, in the abstract. Men are but pawns, their will is but their possible moves, and it is what remains forever alien to them (the *abstractum*) which moves them. Man's significance consists only of this, that the game cannot be played without him, that men are the only possible hieroglyphs with which the mysterious inscription may be composed. . . .(p. 151.)

This is such an umbrella passage that it effectively covers everything between Hebbel and Beckett; hence it is not very useful as a means of isolating subtraditions in modern drama. I cite it, however, because one can see how the structure of the imposed situation (that is, the protagonist as "pawn") in modern drama is a variation of an indispensable plot-form dating back to the Greeks. Screen out certain peculiarly modern overtones, beginning with the nature of the *abstractum,* and the passage applies about as well to Orestes as it does to Marguerite in *La Dame aux camelias*.[8]

I would not insist on as clear a distinction between the two plots of *Godot* as I have drawn out rather severely here; for one thing, as we shall see, there is considerable blending of their energies in the second act. Nor is this the only way to view their differences. In fact, another, and more theological, perspective on what I have been saying is suggested by Kenneth Burke's essay on "The First Three Chapters of Genesis" in *The Rhetoric of Religion*. Burke is here trying to demonstrate how biblical narrative style in Genesis expresses the idea of "original" versus "actual" sin. He distinguishes two styles which he calls the circular and the rectilinear. Another word for circular, he says, might be mythic in that myth "is characteristically a terminology of quasi-narrative terms for the expressing of relationships that are not intrinsically narrative, but 'circular' or 'tautological.'"[9] Thus, the

8. Perhaps the play that most clearly lives up to this "prophesy" is Tom Stoppard's *Rosencrantz and Guildenstern Are Dead* which is literally about what happens when "the baser nature" becomes the "intersection point" of mighty opposites. For illustration purposes, we might retitle it *Didi and Gogo Meet Hamlet*: not only does it lean heavily on *Godot's* characterizations and devices of style, but it brings into clear focus *Godot's* structural underpinnings of a classical tragedy unfolding in the context of modern alienation. Here we see just where Hamlet, that great asker of modern questions, has led us—to a complete dissolution of the *act* as a statement of will. Quite apart from its own merits as a play, *Rosencrantz and Guildenstern* is also an astute piece of Existentialist criticism from the post-*Godot* era. It seems to say: "This is what Beckett has shown us. This is how we would rewrite the Renaissance!"

9. *The Rhetoric of Religion: Studies in Logology* (Berkeley and Los Angeles: University of California Press, 1970), p. 258. Burke repeatedly uses the word *style* in this essay, and as far as I can see he is

Vladimir/Estragon plot is tautological in that it tells the same story twice: the repetition of the structure of Act I in Act II serves, continually, to renew past time, in much the same way that the Cain/Abel story is renewed in the stories of Jacob and Esau and the two thieves. From the perspective of man's situation as a "waiting" creature fallen from God this is the perfect form for expressing conclusively the fact that nothing has changed, that the original conditions still obtain, that man endlessly commits the sin of Adam and therefore endlessly enacts the Crucifixion.

---

not referring to literary style but to different "logological" perspectives one might take on the same image or incident in the Bible, or on the Bible as a whole. For instance: "Thus, where the Scofield Bible comments, 'The history of Israel in the wilderness and in the land is one long record of the violation of the law,' we should interpret this logologically to mean that the Biblical narrative is but continually restating the principle of circularity intrinsic to the idea of Order, continually coming upon this circular situation despite the rectilinearity of the narrative method" (p. 224). In other words, it is not a question of the style of the *text* (in, for instance, Auerbach's use of the term *style*), but of one's perspective on the text. Maybe not. In any case, the point needs clarification inasmuch as I am adjusting Burke's idea to suit a more literary use of the word *style*. In fact, what I have said about the two plots of *Godot* more closely follows Burke's principles of style as set forth in *Counter-Statement*. That is, the "cyclical" style is an exercise in Qualitative Progression, or maintaining the same principle (waiting) under different guises (Act II qualitatively repeats Act I); and the "rectilinear" style is an exercise in Syllogistic Progression, which moves *from* something, *through* something, *to* something quite different (the "drama" of Pozzo and Lucky). The idea would be that any story (say, Cain and Abel) would be a rectilinear narrative, but considered in the context of other stories of grace-given and grace-withheld (say, Jacob and Esau, the two thieves) it would be a circular tautology.

The rectilinear style, on the other hand, is a narrative unfolding, a temporal progression that embodies the larger biblical premise of a Grand Denouement of the world's drama ("a linear progression to end all linear progressions," as Burke says). To come back to my earlier point, we might think of Beckett's narrative problem in *Godot* as being essentially a biblical one: how to keep the Vladimir/Estragon situation from becoming a tautological bore; how, in short, to give this circularity enough linear drive to make it interesting without compromising the all-important theme that the essential doesn't change. To this end, Pozzo and Lucky give the play a considerable narrative boost: theirs is the drama of man's "charge" through time; they are the personifications of historical motion and thrust, of becoming, of man burdened with the baggage of a sinful past and bound for a future which will come, like the Judgment, when they least expect it. Put side by side as purely temporal rhythms, these two plots also have something of the same relationship that tragedy has to the history play: tragedy (the isolation and death of the hero) completes its action, implying that everything that is important happens one fatal time; the history play (the trials of the nation, or race) implies a fresh beginning in every ending (often with a new trouble rising, like Richard Crookback, from the ashes of temporary victory), and assures us that what has been done will have to be done again and again.

I have perhaps put too much stress on the serious side of the play at the expense of the comic. In one connection I likened the Vladimir/Estragon plot to a vaudeville routine, a standard interpretation, and in another to the revenge drama of Orestes and Hamlet. I hope this is not the absurdity it seems, but the reader may wonder how he is supposed to get from the music hall to the palace. So some directions may be in order: in terms of pure organizational mechanics, the Vladimir/Estragon plot is a routine in every sense of the word; that is, it is built up out of improvisational "numbers" which, if nothing else, at least entertain the comedians. Enough has been made of this point in the criticism, but I might recall here Robbe-Grillet's idea that the two tramps are like actors left on stage without "the support of a prepared and carefully learned text."[10] As a consequence, "they must invent," and in the act of inventing they "explain themselves," which is to say, they explain *us*. As for Orestes and Hamlet, I was thinking not of plot organization, but of a general situational likeness. To follow the theatre metaphor further, why are Vladimir and Estragon "on stage" at all if not as a command performance of a god for whom the universe itself is a spectacle of "poor players" (a *theatrum mundi*), a dark theology analogized in the play's earthly terms by Pozzo's command to Lucky, "Think pig!" This "imposed situation" is paralleled by the Ghost's command to Hamlet to "Stir in this, . . . if thou hast nature in thee," and followed up in Hamlet himself not by a swift act of revenge but in acts of delay by which he "explains" the temperamental reasons why he cannot sweep to his revenge. This is what I had in mind (Chapter 1) in saying that *Hamlet*

10. "Samuel Beckett, or 'Presence' in the Theatre," *Samuel Beckett: A Collection of Critical Essays,* ed. Martin Esslin (Englewood Cliffs, N.J.: Prentice-Hall, 1965), p. 113.

and *Godot,* however different otherwise, were treating similar thematic issues. For it seems to me that the improvisational nature of *Hamlet*'s plot is the logical form for exploring the nature of an act (and its act-er) that is morally and existentially problematical. The playwright invents a series of "diversions" which make the delay (or the wait) plausible, while keeping us in suspense as to the outcome. I have always found it interesting that Tom Stoppard, in rewriting *Hamlet* for an audience brought up on Beckett, should reduce its hero to a man of action, "as swift as meditation," and give his more lethargic and speculative characteristics to Ros and Guil who are in the very same dilemma as Vladimir and Estragon in having an incomplete scenario on which to improvise their fate. Or at least they think they are improvising it; as we know, it is being improvised for them by Claudius and Hamlet.

To come at the problem of the play's mixture of comedy and tragedy from still another angle, I might cite a passage from Schopenhauer as an inadvertent comment on *Godot*:

The life of every individual, viewed as a whole and in general, and when only its most significant features are emphasized, is really a tragedy; but gone through in detail it has the character of a comedy. For the doings and worries of the day, the restless mockeries of the moment, the desires and fears of the week, the mishaps of every hour, are all brought about by chance that is always bent on some mischievous trick; they are nothing but scenes from a comedy. The never-fulfilled wishes, the frustrated efforts, the hopes mercilessly blighted by fate, the unfortunate mistakes of the whole life, with increasing suffering and death at the end, always give us a tragedy. Thus, as if fate wished to add mockery to the misery of our existence, our life must contain all the woes of tragedy, and yet we cannot even assert the dignity of tragic characters, but, in the broad detail of life, are inevitably the foolish characters of a comedy.[11]

Obviously even the comic part of life is not funny for Schopenhauer. But, looking at *Godot* "as a whole," Pozzo's and Lucky's tragedy fades into the larger "tragedy" of all humanity, represented by the unrewarded vigil of Vladimir and Estragon. It is not, of course, a tragedy in any technical sense, but it *is* serious: it takes up all those issues with which tragedy is concerned, even death itself (in the metaphor of the gravedigger-obstetrician). But if we go through the play "in detail" this same general structure yields a series of "scenes from a comedy" involving the doings and worries of the day, the mockeries of the moment, desires, fears, and mishaps, all seemingly brought on by chance.

These seem to me the main structural dynamics of the two plots of *Godot*. Moving a step back, we might notice, in conclusion, that in the important respects the play is following the principles of good plot construction beneath all its modern liberties with form; for these two deep structures, in their rhythmic interplay, create (to recall Kermode's terms) an overall or synchronic *tick-tock:* the "waiting" of Vladimir and Estragon produces a "lively expectation" of Pozzo and

11. *The World as Will and Representation,* trans. E. F. J. Payne (New York: Dover Publications, 1966), I: 322.

Lucky (an arrival of some sort) and they, in turn, help to bestow upon the play both its duration (a closure of its openness) and its meaning. Our final problem is to see just how this happens, what peculiar chemistry takes place when these two energies collide in the last act of the play.

VI
Perhaps

Some years ago, J. I. M. Stewart suggested that the source of psychological depth in Shakespeare's heroes arose from his having contrived to leave the motives obscure, if not self-contradictory.[1] In effect, he was describing the painter's principle of *sfumato* writ large: in the gaps between the articulated possibilities we infer a depth that is not there, or more correctly, a depth that articulation would only violate, make shallow. This is the great frustration in writing about *Godot:* the inevitable problem of isolating the play's possibilities, especially the self-contradictory ones (i.e., Godot arrives and he does not arrive), is that the gap disappears and one emerges with the articulated alternatives that only contain the mystery taking place *in* the gap. Beckett's fondness for the "shape" of the parable of the two thieves suggests what interpretive criticism is bound to miss: the undefinable power that is released when two clear and opposed statements are brought into perfect symmetry. You do not simply have damnation and/or salvation but a portable model of the world's capacity to consternate.

Still, if there is evidence that the idea in the parable of the thieves is one Beckett does not "believe in," that he

1. J. I. M. Stewart, *Character and Motive in Shakespeare: Some Recent Appraisals Examined* (London: Longmans, 1959), p. 96.

has written the whole question off as irrelevant, it is not to be found in the play he wrote on the subject. For Augustine, the idea was only a sometime paradox; it was, in short, a clear revelation of God's unfathomability. Grace is not something one earns by "good works" or faith but by having been elected by God "for reasons unknown" and time will never tell because time is a strictly human, and therefore insufficient, construct for measuring the "things" of God. For Beckett, the parable of the thieves was a paradox of a different order. For one thing, the percentages are made even riskier by the fact that one must rely on conflicting eyewitness accounts. Only two of the Evangelists who were there, or thereabouts, even mention thieves and, of the two, one takes the hard line that both thieves abused Christ, which, by Vladimir's calculation, packs them both off to hell. In other words, the paradox is itself nested in paradox; things begin to look more and more like Kafka's parable of the Doorkeeper in which the "way in" is barred by progressively more abominable guards. The fact is, it is no longer a question of which half of us God inexplicably loves dearly but of the more basic (that is to say, modern) question of God's very existence. Thus, the two thieves come to stand for the alternatives of a possible heavenly salvation with a *possible* God, on one hand, or a total "damnation" in the endless night of the abyssal depths, on the other. In the context of modern Angst (and Beckett's later work) it is possible to read *Godot* as an affirmation of the latter, but the play itself is poised between the alternatives and leaves it an open question.

As it happens, Beckett has given us an interpretation of his play along these same dialectical lines, and while it is scarcely proof of what we have in the play, it would be in order to cite it here:

If life and death did not both present themselves to us, there would be no inscrutability. If there were only darkness, all would be clear. It is because there is not only darkness but also light that our situation becomes inexplicable. Take Augustine's doctrine of grace given and grace withheld: have you pondered the dramatic qualities of this theology? Two thieves are crucified with Christ, one saved and the other damned. How can we make sense of this division? In classical drama, such problems do not arise. The destiny of Racine's Phedre is sealed from the beginning: she will proceed into the dark. As she goes, she herself will be illuminated. At the beginning of the play she has partial illumination and at the end she has complete illumination, but there has been no question but that she moves toward the dark. That is the play. Within this notion clarity is possible, but for us who are neither Greek nor Jansenist there is not such clarity. The question would also be removed if we believed in the contrary—total salvation. But where we have both dark and light we have also the inexplicable. The key word in my plays is "perhaps."[2]

It could hardly matter less that Beckett is referring to his "plays" in the plural. In terms of what I have been saying about *Godot,* I would gloss his commentary as follows: Vladimir and Estragon stand for the "we," two moderns befogged in the inexplicable grayness of

2. Interview with Tom Driver, "Beckett by the Madeleine," *Columbia University Forum* 4, No. 3 (Summer 1961): 23.

"perhaps." Pozzo is Phedre: a relic, an anachronism, an erstwhile truth—but even so the logical historical argument to the contrary. That is, if one were posing a contrast that would illustrate how far we have come from an accountable universe, it might be the dark world of tragedy which has, at least, the comfort of being designed and instructive. Pozzo's destiny, like Phedre's, is sealed from the beginning (from the "Night" speech); he proceeds into the dark, and though we do not see the scene, we presume that "as he goes" he is illuminated. I am assuming that what Beckett means by "illumination" is the process by which the tragic hero is made aware, either gradually (like Macbeth) or suddenly (like Oedipus) of what the journey into the dark means. In other words, tragedy is "a complex act of clarification."[3] In Pozzo this act is condensed into one speech in which he stands outside time in a brief space of temporal integration. What he says is that all crises, from the coming hither to the going hence, take place in the same second. The light gleams an instant, then it is night once more.

Exactly what does this speech mean, in the play's own terms? It is often argued that despite the speech Pozzo goes blindly out of the play, ego-bound to the end. I have no interest in dignifying him further than I have, but it seems important to distinguish between what a character achieves for himself and what he

3. This phrase appears in Morton Gurewitch's *Comedy: The Irrational Vision* (Ithaca, N.Y.: Cornell University Press, 1975), p. 84. For a complete discussion of this view of tragedy (which Gurewitch reviews) see Scott Buchanan, *Poetry and Mathematics* (Philadelphia and New York: J. B. Lippincott Company, 1962), pp. 142–156.

achieves for the play and its audience; and from this standpoint Pozzo's closing words on stage are the crucial hinge on which the play turns.

I have compared it to certain "time" speeches in Shakespeare, but the fact that Shakespeare often has his heroes sum up their lives in such terms suggests that he was appropriating a conventional Renaissance idea and tailoring it to the needs of tragedy. In any case, Shakespeare's conclusions about time, and actions done in it, are not Beckett's. We are further along if we return to Augustine. I have in mind specifically his famous contrast of God's time ("Thy years are one day, . . . thy today is eternity") and man's time, divided into *memory* ("the present of things past"), *sight* ("the present of things present"), and *expectation* ("the present of things future").[4] What is lost in any reduction of Augustine's thought on this "most entangled enigma" is the relentlessness of his inquiry in the face of its agonizing question: How may one measure time? *What* has one measured? Since the agony of the question is as important as the answer itself, I offer this passage as a sample:

Suffer me, O Lord, to seek further; O my hope, let not my purpose be confounded. For if there are times past and fu-

4. From "The Confessions," *An Augustine Reader,* ed. John J. O'Meara (Garden City, N.Y.: Doubleday, 1973), pp. 187, 192. In what follows I hope it is clear that I am using Augustine as an analogous text, with no inference that it is, in any sense, a source for *Godot.* It is logical to assume that Beckett was familiar with the famous "time" discussion in the *Confessions*; but Augustine's ideas about time are scarcely unique, however testimonial of his own warmth and tenacity as a paradoxist doing the work of God on earth. The truth is, whole passages do leap out of Augustine, almost as if they were sources, until one realizes that Beckett could have absorbed the ideas from any number of commentaries on the

ture I desire to know where they are. But if as yet I do not succeed, I still know, wherever they are, that they are not there as future or past, but as present. For if there also they be future, they are not as yet there; if even there they be past, they are no longer there. Wherever, therefore, they are, whatever they are, they are only so as present. Although past things are related as true, they are drawn out from the memory,—not the things themselves, which have passed, but the words conceived from the images of the things which they have formed in the mind as footprints in their passage through the senses (pp. 190–191).

The upshot of this problem is that man is unavoidably "divided amid times" and life becomes "a distraction" spent between "things that are past" and "things which shall be and shall pass away" (p. 201). This is the essential frustration on which our play discourses— without, of course, coming to Augustine's spiritual conclusion. The lives of Vladimir and Estragon, particularly, act out an obsessive displacement of time. The "homesickness" for a perdurable present, expressed so poignantly by Augustine and experienced at rare moments by every human being, is simply not

---

Scriptures or on the subject of time. There is another way in which we may be misled into finding parallels in their work. In his little essay on Kafka, Borges says that "Every writer *creates* his own precursors. His work modifies our conception of the past, as it will modify the future." The early Kafka of *Betrachtung*, Borges argues, is less a precursor of the Kafka of "sombre myths and atrocious institutions" than is the Browning of "Fears and Scruples" and the Lord Dunsany of "Carcassonne" (*Labyrinths: Selected Stories and Other Writings* [n.p.: Penguin Books, 1974], p. 236). In this sense, Augustine is the "created" precursor of Beckett (or is it *vice versa?*) in that Augustine's work is "perceptibly sharpen[ed] and deflect-[ed]" if read by Beckett twilight.

theirs. The present (of things present) is a monster to be slain, an encumbrance (as the body is for certain mystics), above all a medium of diversion in which *being* is centrifugally spun out into what *was* ("What exactly did we ask him for?") and what *will be* ("We'll hang ourselves tomorrow"). Thus, forever shuttling between memory and expectation, they carry to the extreme the condition in which all normal life is lived.

The best way to integrate Pozzo into this time scheme is to summarize once more the two stages of his career, this time from an Augustinian perspective. In Act I, as I have said, his symbol is the watch which at one point is casually mistaken for his heart. Readers have noted his likeness to the March Hare, but he is a much bigger entrepreneur of time than that. His "charge" through space (recalling, again, Tamburlaine) has the character of a conquest of time, as if time had some external validity and substance that could be stored in Lucky's bags or annexed, like land, according to how much a man can cover on foot in a day.[5] His

5. The very idea of a half-hunter with deadbeat escapement (not simply a watch) carries the bourgeois' pride in ownership of an efficient machine, as Lewis Mumford puts it, "whose 'product' is seconds and minutes." "The clock, not the steam-engine, is the key machine of the modern industrial age. For every phase of its development the clock is both the outstanding fact and the typical symbol of the machine." With an eye on the clock, one does not spend time, one saves it; though it passes away, one has measured it, as a meter measures the flow of water and saves, at least, the memory of the water (which, in the world of trade, is as good as the thing itself). Thus time, since the clock, ceases to be a "sequence of experiences" and becomes "a collection of hours" (from *Technics and Civilization* [New York: Harcourt, Brace and Co., 1934], pp. 15–17, *passim*).

"Night" speech is the virtual antithesis of Augustine's painful deliberation on whether the day (time itself) is constituted by the circuit of the sun from east to west or by the period in which the circuit is completed. Or is it both? Or neither? The enigma repeatedly throws Augustine on God's mercy and to the end he remains "ignorant as to what time is" (p. 196). For Pozzo it is not an enigma at all but a simple problem of calculation on the half-hunter. For him, time is visibly coextensive with nature's processes and it can be harnessed, or at least monitored, by the watch. When Vladimir says, "Time has stopped," Pozzo cuddles his watch to his ear in a remarkable confusion of means and ends ("Whatever you like, but not that"). Motion is time flushed out, caught in the act of stealing away, and what apparently makes night his primal fear is that it eclipses all the signs by which time (in bourgeois parlance) is "kept honest" and questions like Augustine's do not arise. There is something Proustian about his dread of night, if one recalls Proust's experience of awakening in the dark and discovering, in a great "hammer-blow," that one is without history, duration, or substance: a consciousness in a void.

In Act II, Pozzo's symbol is sand, which belongs by the common consent of poets to the world of Time. It also has "solemn human resonances" (Kenner's phrase) of burden and punishment, Sisyphus and Atlas (though Lucky is still the goat), but above all, sand is an endless, undifferentiated, final form, the hard proof of earth's passage through time; it is, in fact, the nearest thing to entropic "realization" that we have. All told, the categorical opposite of the watch and the perfect metronome to accompany the "feeble apocalypse" of the "When!" speech—which, in effect, is a restatement (without the solace of God's mercy) of Augustine's perception that time is "of the mind itself," nothing but "protraction, but of what I know not" (p. 197).

Actually, Pozzo might have answered Vladimir's question ("Since when?") even more philosophically by quoting one of Beckett's favorite secular thinkers: "Our own past," Schopenhauer says, "even the most recent, even the previous day, is only an empty dream of the imagination. . . . What was? What is? . . . Future and past are only in the concept. . . . No man has lived in the past, and none will ever live in the future; the *present* alone is the form of all life. . . ."[6] This is not exactly what Pozzo means, but the "When!" speech comes down to some such abandonment, or loss, of those comforting categories of past and future by which man grounds his life in a personal continuity. Symptomatically, Pozzo's "defective" memory of Act I is even further deteriorated in Act II. He recalls evening and a place called the Board, but otherwise his mind is a self-erasing tablet.

There is another parallel with Proust that suggests larger implications of amnesia in the *Godot* world. "In Proustian thought," Georges Poulet writes, "memory plays the same supernatural role as grace in Christian thought. It is this inexplicable phenomenon that comes

6. *The World as Will and Representation*, trans. E. F. J. Payne (New York: Dover Publications, 1966), I: 278. I have somewhat shuffled the order of Schopenhauer's thought, for my own emphasis.

to apply itself to a fallen nature, irremediably separated from its origins, not to restore it integrally and at once to its first condition, but to give it the efficacy to find the highway of its salvation. Remembrance is the 'succour from on high' which comes to the being in order 'to draw him from the nothingness out of which, by himself, he would not have been able to emerge.'"[7] Where time is concerned, parallels with Proust come rather easily, given Beckett's own interest and the fact that Proust wrote what amounts to an encyclopedia on the subject of memory. But it really was not necessary to quote Poulet to see this connection. He simply makes it more accessible than, say, Beckett's own book on Proust in which memory is described as "the Old Testament of the individual" (p. 19) and life as "a succession of Paradises successively denied" (p. 14). In any event, on simple dramatic grounds, there is good reason to see loss of memory as a metaphor for the fall from grace. Vladimir and Estragon act out the parallel continually in questions like "What exactly did we ask him for?" and "Were you not there?" Moreover, Pozzo's fall into forgetfulness, in its contour, is a virtual reenactment (or play-within-a-play) of the greater Fall which gives the drama of waiting its *raison d'être*. That is, as the play opens, the fall of Vladimir and Estragon has already occurred, being synonymous with the Fall of man (at least on the theological side of the play's question). But as the Fall is successively enacted, Paradise successively denied, it occurs again before our

7. Georges Poulet, *Studies in Human Time,* trans. Elliott Coleman (Baltimore and London: Johns Hopkins Press, 1970), p. 297.

eyes in Pozzo, producing the effect of a flashback. As
Santayana says, what man forgets he is destined to
repeat.

In the peculiar logic of symbolism these "falls" are
in turn reflected sensuously in the play's overall imagery in much the same way that murder in *Hamlet* is
reflected in the imagery of blasted flowers, burning
loins, and maggot-stuffed dogs. Most of the key images participate, in one way or another, in the dialectic
of grace-given and grace-withheld. The scenic equiva-
lents of these opposing concepts are probably "day"
and "night" which belong respectively, to "grace" and
"damnation." Under them we could list others, such
as:

Day (Grace)	*Night (Damnation)*
light (sun)	dark (moon)
fire	cold
sight	blindness
waking	sleeping
birth	death
world	void
watch	sand
memory	amnesia

And for good measure, we might put one of Estragon's boots on either side of the ledger. In a sense, most
of these are conventional literary oppositions. Some of
them are admittedly "twilight" terms that could belong to either column: "sight" may, in fact, be "blindness" if one is seeing the wrong thing; birth may equal
death, if as Pozzo says, both occur at the same mo-

ment; the world may be conceived as the void; and one may burn in the "great cold" of damnation. But such conversions are always a function of the context in which the image appears and the play usually makes this clear or implies that both readings may be implicit in the image. In any event, I think we have no choice but to put *amnesia* in the grace-withheld column. It is a condition that somehow attends blindness, which somehow attends the bursting of night, death, the void, and the transportation of sand. In other words, if an author makes a point about failing memory in a play dealing with salvation and damnation, and repeatedly makes it on the damnation side of the scale, the two become consubstantial.[8]

This is something of the philosophical resonance of Pozzo's blindness. What we want to know now is

8. For a complete treatment of such oppositions in Beckett, see James Knowlson, *Light and Darkness in the Theatre of Samuel Beckett* (London: Turret Books, 1972). It should be said that the argument here is not that amnesia is a condition necessarily inflicted by a god. There is also the sense in which the concept of Godot (and Grace) may represent the secular goal of self-realization, something very much like *virtu* (the thing at the peak of its natural being). As Schopenhauer says, in *potentia* every person is Adam as well as Christ, "according as he comprehends himself, and his will thereupon determines him" (II: 628). One of the fascinating ambiguities of the play, in fact, is that Godot is constantly, and elusively, popping up as *both* self-determination and as divine command, when you think you have only one or the other; the ironic result is that, though both are contained in the same "shape," one is a correction, or even a refutation, of the other. The parable of the thieves all over. Anyway, what may be grace in a divinely ordained world is something else in a humanistic one. Either way, memory is, as Poulet says, "the highway" to either goal and it is in a bad state of disrepair in this play.

what use the play makes of this event. And it would be helpful to begin by returning to Schopenhauer. In the same discussion from which I have quoted, Schopenhauer goes on to compare time to a sphere that is constantly revolving against a tangent: "The half that is always sinking would be the past, and the half that is always rising would be the future; but at the top, the indivisible point that touches the tangent would be the extensionless present. Just as the tangent does not continue rolling with the sphere, so also the present, the point of contact of the object whose form is time, does not roll on with the subject that has no form, since it does not belong to the knowable, but is the condition of all that is knowable" (pp. 279–280). This analogy returns us by a different route to my diagram of the circle and the pyramid representing the play's two plots in collision. Rethinking the diagram now as a model of the play's time-structure, we could substitute Schopenhauer tangents for the slopes of the Pozzo/ Lucky pyramid which, on successive "days," touch the "revolving sphere" of the Vladimir/Estragon continuum. The two "days" of the play would now look like this:

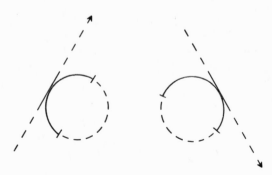

The points of contact, of course, are not points at all but entire scenes. But these scenes accomplish, in dramatic terms, the effect of an "indivisible point" of *presence* which is "the condition of all that is knowable," in the play as out of it. We are looking at the sphere now not as a circular or tautological plot but as the state of Vladimir's and Estragon's time-consciousness, constantly rising toward the future (expectation) and falling into the past (memory), with no repose in a *now*. With the arrival of Pozzo and Lucky on each day it is momentarily exposed to an event of passing time, an extended *now*, that is in dramatic counterpoint to the rhythm of "waiting." In Act I, this event is very simply absorbed into the routine as a more exciting species of diversion than the tree, the boots, and the surrounding muck. Vladimir and Estragon are entertained by the company of men, given bones, talked to about this and that; the twilight is explained, and they have a sample of "thought." All this passes the time; which would have passed in any case; but no so rapidly. Thus the play establishes the pattern by which its protagonists habitually relate to the passing world, a world that the "entertainment" has invited us to associate metaphorically with larger celestial rhythms.

This is substantially the case in Act II, with a crucial difference. It would have been easy enough to reincorporate Pozzo and Lucky into the routine, as a juggler might add another ball to the cascade or as Estragon's beatings are incorporated into the ritual of night. But they have "changed"; they have not lived up to memory. Time, says Schopenhauer, "is the mere possibility of opposed states in the same matter" (p. 135), which is also a definition of tragic reversal. In tragedy, the movement to the "opposed state," into the dark, passes through an extended twilight; but in Pozzo's and Lucky's case we have only the flat juxtaposition of the light and the dark. They have become, instantaneously, as it were, the products of time. Here, for once, the world throws up queer proof of its existence (and we may note, in passing, how the tree has anticipated this event by realizing the "possibilities" of its own matter).

To move a step back, the problem I raised at the end of the last chapter might be restated like this: how can this unending play be brought to a close, not only in the normal interests of dramatic climax but of putting the issue raised by its title into the most final possible perspective? What was needed was an electrifying moment, not precisely of insight but of incisiveness, something that might bite into the smug circle of routine and bring, at least, the jolting realization that there *are* "points" of expressiveness in the continuum. The moment in which this occurs is the play's master peripety (parallel to the Herdsman's *coup de grace* in *Oedipus Rex:* "If you are the man he says you are . . . ."). To be precise, I would set it in these lines:

Vladimir:	Before you go tell him to sing.
Pozzo:	Who?
Vladimir:	Lucky.
Pozzo:	To sing?
Vladimir:	Yes. Or to think. Or to recite.
Pozzo:	But he is dumb.

Vladimir: Dumb!
  Pozzo: Dumb. He can't even groan.
Vladimir: Dumb! Since when?

The point is not that Lucky's fate is more important
than Pozzo's (though from Vladimir's viewpoint a
case could be made for this idea), but that in these lines
the action of time, or Fate, is shown to have been fully
symmetrical, beyond chance: the *comble* is complete.
All in all, it has the character of a bizarre accident, the
terror of which lies in an uncanny precision (as of
lightning striking twice). The onlooker, hypothetical
victim himself, must now recreate the event, draw it
back into the safety of the gratuitous, the coin-
cidental—that is, the normal. And this is the sense of
the question, "Since when?"—involuntary, in these
cases, as the flinch of an eye.

    There is another face of causality of the Pozzo/Lucky
disaster that bears on their becoming "products of
time" and on what I take to be Vladimir's horrified
reaction to the news that Lucky is dumb. If time is the
mere possibility of opposed states in the same matter,
space, Schopenhauer goes on to say, is "the mere possibility of the persistence of the same matter in all kinds
of opposed states." The union of time and space thus
shows itself as the principle of causality, or becoming.
It seems to me that in the suddenness of accident we
have our clearest proof of time's process. What happens to us emotionally at the scene of a highway accident, for example, is not a simple and sympathetic
revolt of the flesh at the sight of blood, but the more
awful fact that the wheels of the upturned vehicle are

still turning: nature has shown no sympathy for the "tragedy"; time has not stopped at the moment of impact. In this continuance of the mundane one suddenly sees the very cause of things, a grand democratic principle in nature wherein all things are subject to the same gains and losses, the same invisible laws that have to do only coincidentally with human designs. The straight line of the victim's journey has been abruptly broken off ("Where was he going?") by another plan in progress (fatigue? a defective machine?). There is a scene in *War and Peace* that catches this idea perfectly: a Russian factory worker stands bound and blindfolded before a French firing squad. The rifles are cocked and the command about to be given. But the wily Tolstoi, who wrote that history is the sum of the infinitesimal tendencies of men, adds a ghastly detail to his scene: as the lad's flesh girds for the volley, his position against the bloodstained post becomes "uncomfortable" and, involuntarily, he shifts his weight, human to the end. In the scene I am discussing, the arrival of Pozzo and Lucky, blind and dumb, presents us with something like this sudden confluence of radically different plans in nature. In *Proust,* Beckett says that "suffering opens a window on the real" (p. 16): here the real suddenly injects itself into the routine and provides the jolt that brings Vladimir, the "waiter," to his senses.[9]

9. Couldn't we say, by the same token, that almost any event in any play is subject to this same causal system, that we are doing nothing more than applying self-evident laws of physics to a human drama? Yes: except that this particular instance of the "accidental," of becoming, is the climactic episode of a play that has spent most of its time avoiding the world of change, showing the persistence of the "same matter" in the same state. Consider, as a parallel example, how Chekhov, Beckett's natural "precursor" in

As we have seen, Vladimir's question ("Since when?") receives an answer that invalidates the very principle of duration; and the scene that follows may be described as a slow sinking in of the shock. From this moment the play becomes oddly straightforward: there is no more oxymoronic gap between words and implications. What Vladimir gets from Pozzo and Lucky is not clear, but it amounts to a deep suspicion that he has been in the presence of an event that somehow puts waiting into a new orientation. Suffering opens a window on the real—meaning, one gathers, that the real cannot be seen in the familiar because it has iterated itself out of sight; it is also an argument dating back to Ivan Karamazov that suffering is the one indisputable fact of life that makes the promise of grace in the hereafter a debatable reward. In any event, Pozzo's words leave their mark and, with his departure into the void, the stage is set for the play's most complex moment.[10]

---

the drama of Time, produces the same effect in *The Cherry Orchard*: nothing, no amount of logic or persuasion from Lopahin, will convince Lyubov's family that disaster is in the offing if they do not sell the orchard. Perhaps they know it, or may even be inviting the disaster suicidally, at some unexpressed level. But the play is bent upon analyzing the condition of persistence, turning one's back on the world of change, on the real. Yet, as Faustus says, time *will* run, the clock *will* strike. And the axe blow that falls, throwing two orders of time (the nineteenth and the twentieth centuries) in collision, is Lopahin's single line: "*I* bought it!"

10. In this connection, the second crucifixion scene in which Vladimir and Estragon support Pozzo on either side is the natural preface to a scene that has given us, as its climactic tension, the arrival of suffering in a world so obsessed with things-to-come that the present threatens to be emptied of all value. To the reader who may resist the idea that this is a crucifixion scene at all, I would add

In one sense, Vladimir's soliloquy is a classic recognition speech which sums up the career in waiting exactly as the "When!" speech sums up Pozzo's career in becoming. But it is also close to what Northrop Frye calls the *Augenblick* of tragedy, that "crucial moment from which point the road to what might have been and the road to what will be can be simultaneously seen":[11]

Was I sleeping while the others suffered? Am I sleeping now? To-morrow, when I wake, or think I do, what shall I say of to-day? That with Estragon my friend, at this place, until the fall of night, I waited for Godot? That Pozzo passed, with his carrier, and that he spoke to us? Probably.

---

that it does not depend upon seeing Pozzo as Christ or on a religious assumption that God, or Godot, has arrived "in spirit." The play has simply impressed the form of a crucifixion on its matter as a means of focusing our responses, if only subliminally. One could interpret it in many ways. An Augustinian Christian might claim that the "hand" of God, at least, is present in the scene. God being, as Augustine says, both interior and exterior to all things: the scene is thus an opportunity for the tramps to "realize" God. On the other side, an Athiest, or Christian-in-principle-only, like Camus, would argue that Christ has arrived in the only form man deserves: a fellow-sufferer calling for help. The idea would be that waiting is misguided, that the tramps are "lying" to themselves in bringing in a hope "which means nothing within the limits of [their] condition," as Camus says in *The Myth of Sisyphus*. This scene proves that their priorities are incorrect. In fact, as a mythic construct, the scene would illustrate any number of texts on the subject of misguided "future" complexes, from E. M. Cioran's *The New Gods* to Henry James's "The Beast in the Jungle," the story of a man who in waiting for his "destiny" (for something "special" to happen to him) fails to recognize the destiny when it arrives.
11. *Anatomy of Criticism,* (Princeton, N.J.: Princeton University Press, 1957) p. 213.

But in all that what truth will there be? *(Estragon, having struggled with his boots in vain, is dozing off again. Vladimir looks at him.)* He'll know nothing. He'll tell me about the blows he received and I'll give him a carrot. *(Pause.)* Astride of a grave and a difficult birth. Down in the hole, lingeringly, the grave-digger puts on the forceps. We have time to grow old. The air is full of our cries. *(He listens.)* But habit is a great deadener. *(He looks again at Estragon.)* At me too someone is looking, of me too someone is saying, He is sleeping, he knows nothing, let him sleep on. *(Pause.)* I can't go on! *(Pause.)* What have I said?

This is an ingenious adaptation of tragedy's trigger mechanism to the play's own cathartic ends. In sum, we have a two-stage recognition: the first (the "When!" speech) is partial, more illuminating than il-luminated; this is the second, built upon the findings of the first and combined, as I have said, with the play's peripety in good classical fashion.[12] In fact, discarding differences in tone and character, one can read the two speeches without interrruption as complementary phases of the same idea. Vladimir fulfills Pozzo's thought not only in recovering his "grave" metaphor but in stretching his perception that life passes in "an instant" into something like a moral question. Here the important themes of the play (sleep, blindness, suf-fering, night, waiting, death, time) are drawn into an interrogative suspension. What is remarkable is the lucidity of mind with which Vladimir looks back upon "today" from the perspective of "to-morrow" (a

12. Vivian Mercier makes an interesting case for a "classical" (and specifically Racinian) influence on Beckett's plays in *Beckett/Beckett* (New York: Oxford University Press, 1977), p. 73ff.

complex act in this play) and searches its experience for a "truth." This is the only moment in the play when Vladimir speaks to and of himself in what we might call the past-future tense. It is, in fact, almost a Racinian speech in the sense that a character is contemplating his own destiny before it has been fully worked out. Here Vladimir, like Pozzo, stands outside himself, at a cross-road, a consciousness momentarily detached from the "habit" of the body, represented by the sleeping Estragon who serves, at this moment, as a condensation of the whole principle of waiting. Altogether, it is a daring speech, for this play, in coming so close to the point that there may be better ways of spending one's fraction of time on this bitch of an earth.

To a point, I would agree with critics (for instance, Eva Metman[13]) that the arrival of the Boy plunges Vladimir back into the paralysis of waiting—which is to say that he takes the road to "what will be"; but this does not erase the emotional effect of his realization. For in placing Vladimir, however briefly, outside his "pernicious devotion" to habit, allowing him to see it for the great deadener it is, the play has provided an objective perspective on the whole question of waiting. It does not, of course, provide an answer, just as Racine's or Shakespeare's recognitions provide no answer; but it does constitute a long-range assessment of the experience. I would take the line, "At me too someone is looking, . . ." as an open invitation to the audience, overseeing all (and in turn, like Browning's

13. "Reflections on Samuel Beckett's Plays," *Samuel Beckett: A Collection of Critical Essays,* ed. Martin Esslin (Englewood Cliffs, N.J.: Prentice-Hall, 1965), p. 128.

Caliban, being overseen), to make an evaluation of its own; thus the recognition is passed over to the audience who will probably handle it in much the same confused way that Vladimir does.

There is another overtone to the speech that will round out much of what I have been saying about the theme of time. Near the end of his discussion of time, Augustine offers, as a common metaphor of the "enigma," the manner in which the simple repetition of a psalm undergoes a journey through the trinity of human time, passing from expectation (the part of the psalm to be said), through his "consideration" (the present, or point of contact between tangent and sphere: "the condition of all that is knowable"), into memory (what he has already said of the psalm). "And what takes place in the entire psalm," he concludes, "takes place also in each individual part of it, and in each individual syllable: this holds true in the longer action, of which that psalm is perhaps a portion; the same holds true in the whole life of man, of which all the actions of man are parts; the same holds true in the whole age of the sons of men, of which all the lives of men are parts" (pp. 200–201).

The beauty of this analogy is unfortunately not one we can fully share today. But it does put the microsensation of being-in-time into the macro-life of the race. In a very special way, it seems to me that Vladimir's soliloquy enacts this same passage. In it, we literally experience an act of forgetting. For a brief second, Vladimir stands in the present contemplating the meaning of Pozzo's "passing" and asks what truth there may be in "all that." But before his contemplation is over, the lesson can be "heard" retreating into memory. The present proceeds to become "absent," the wheel moves away from the tangent, the cry that filled the air is past and can no longer be measured "because it no longer is." Thus Vladimir is divided, for the first time, amid times; the line "What have I said?" marks his abrupt return to the only zone of comfort he knows; Estragon awakes—eloquent symbol of the rebirth of habit—and mind and body become one again. In this manner the speech suffers its own life in time and in doing so becomes the "part" of the play that most intensely renders the sense in which it is a psalm for the forgetful age of men.

One might argue, of course, that the return to waiting is really a decision prompted by a serious, if disorganized, weighing of the alternatives and that the seed of understanding planted by Pozzo and Lucky will bear fruit in the days to come. Maybe the tree has set a precedent; maybe not. But in this vein, we could submit several proofs. For one, there are those lines, "It seemed to me he saw us" and "Not at all! *(Less sure.)* Not at all! *(Still less sure.)* Not at all!" which suggest that something memorable has happened in this small space of time. Then there is the calmer, more mature—one might even say *athambic*—conduct of the interview with the second Boy, especially the critical line, "Tell him . . . *(he hesitates)* . . . tell him that you saw me and that . . . *(he hesitates)* . . . that you saw me," which suggests a kind of "Let be," or readiness to accept the conditions, whatever they may be, implied by Godot's likely nonappearance tomorrow.

However, I prefer a more ambiguous ending, one

that would include this possibility without endorsing it; for to the extent that the play becomes decisive on this critical ground (and there are risks of sentimentality in a clearly affirmative ending) it gives the lie to what has all along been its premise. In other words, a play cannot say it means "perhaps" or "Nothing is certain" and then proceed to act out a certainty. Like the Augustinian doctrine it must dramatize "perhaps" as a continuing dialectical stalemate between "yes" and "no." As Beckett says, it is the shape that matters, the shape that comes queerly forward as the very proof of the idea. In fact, there is a sense in which the particular idea *in* this shape is but the local exemplum of a whole class of ideas that are not necessarily soteriological or spiritual in implication. For instance, we might set Augustine's doctrine against the "background" of a companion doctrine from philosophy which might serve as a secular epigraph for the play, and for this essay. I am thinking of a proposition attributed to Niels Bohr: "The opposite of an ordinary truth is a falsehood; the opposite of a profound truth is another profound truth."[14] Here is a doctrine, endlessly fascinating and frustrating, which is faithfully acting out its own meaning. We are quickly drawn into the comfortable world of logic and scrutability where $2 + 2 = 4$ is invariably true, and $2 + 1 = 4$ is invariably false.

14. Actually, I have sharpened this proposition for somewhat more paradoxical purposes than Bohr had in mind. His version (or rather, Werner Heisenberg's version of his version) should read: "The opposite of a correct statement is a false statement. But the opposite of a profound truth may well be another profound truth" quoted in Werner Heisenberg's *Physics and Beyond: Encounters and Conversations* [New York: Harper and Row, 1971], p. 102.

We are on safe ground: clarity *is* possible. But this is clearly not a full account of truth, at least not in the fallen world of relativity and antimatter. And just as the universe of logic itself contains the working concepts of both syllogism and paradox, the unforeseen suddenly erupts, like the punch line of a joke, and the bottom of certainty falls out. But only momentarily, for there is something gratifying about having the tables turned on us so precisely. The gratification is not in any truth we might locate in the proposition, but in our having as consolation a verbal structure which mimics, at the dialectical extreme, a universe that will supply "truthful" answers to whatever loaded questions are put to it.

Index